Routledge Revivals

New India

First published in 1909, the purpose of this book was to draw attention to the political, social and religious changes that were taking place in India and detail how this should inform British colonial policy. The author argues that the political situation demanded decisive action as several factors had caused increasing difficulties in administration, including waning enthusiasm on the part of English officials and greater tension between the governors and the governed often caused by colonial arrogance — brought into sharper relief by spread of education and the growth of patriotic feeling. He also argues that the crux of India's economic difficulties was the poverty of its people and asserts that the solution to both problems was the 'sympathetic and systematic encouragement of her legitimate aspirations and patriotic tendencies'. In regard to social and religious changes, the author observes that they were not less considerable and advises that the government should, as far as was possible, maintain the existing basis by a policy of 'wise conservation'. This book will be of interest to students of Indian history and colonialism.

New India

or India in Transition

Henry Cotton

Routledge
Taylor & Francis Group

First published in 1909
by Kegan Paul, Trench, Trübner, & Co.

This edition first published in 2017 by Routledge
2 Park Square, Milton Park, Abingdon, Oxon, OX14 4RN
and by Routledge
711 Third Avenue, New York, NY 10017

Routledge is an imprint of the Taylor & Francis Group, an informa business

Publisher's Note
The publisher has gone to great lengths to ensure the quality of this reprint but points out that some imperfections in the original copies may be apparent.

Disclaimer
The publisher has made every effort to trace copyright holders and welcomes correspondence from those they have been unable to contact.

A Library of Congress record exists under LC control number: 07021293

ISBN 13: 978-1-138-28215-5 (hbk)
ISBN 13: 978-1-315-27080-7 (ebk)
ISBN 13: 978-1-138-28224-7 (pbk)

From a Photograph by
Messrs Johnston & Hoffmann.

Henry Cotton.

NEW INDIA

OR

INDIA IN TRANSITION

BY

SIR HENRY COTTON, K.C.S.I., M.P.

REVISED AND ENLARGED

LONDON
KEGAN PAUL, TRENCH, TRÜBNER, & Co., Ltd.
Dryden House, Gerrard Street, W.
1909

PREFACE

My object in writing this book is to draw attention to the great changes which are taking place in India—changes political, social, and religious—and to the spirit which, in my judgment, should inspire our policy in relation to them.

The political situation demands decisive treatment. The conditions of our occupation combine to show increased difficulties in administration; a waning enthusiasm on the part of English officials, occasioned by a livelier consciousness of the drawbacks of Indian life; and a greater friction between the governors and the governed, attributable to many causes, but especially to the arrogance in thought and language of the ruling race, which has been brought out into stronger relief by the extension of education and the growth of independence and patriotic feeling among the people. Able and energetic Indians, enlightened and educated by ourselves, expanding with new ideas and fired by an ambition to which English education has given birth, make demands which are continually more and more reasonable and more irresistible. The waves of the ocean of Indian progress are dashing against the breakwater of English prejudice. The members of the Anglo-Indian community, like the courtiers of Canute, call loudly on the Government to restrain the advancing tide. The Government, insufficiently attuned to the requirements of the situation, unlike Canute, is not yet strong enough or wise enough to turn a deaf ear to their advice.

India's political problem is the growth of an Indian nation ; her economic problem is the poverty of her people. The solution of the problems lies in the sympathetic and systematic encouragement of her legitimate aspirations and patriotic tendencies. A constructive policy is needed which shall not only guide and control events during the period of transition, but shall also when necessary abstain from interference. The difficulty is to pass from the old to the new order without disturbance.

In their religious and social aspect the changes taking place are not less considerable. The function of Government in this case is to preserve, as far as possible, the existing basis of order by a policy of wise conservation.

Preface

I have confined myself to the discussion of general questions, avoiding detail as much as possible, principally because details are unsuited to the English reader, for whom this book is primarily intended. If I appear to have written strongly, it is because I feel strongly. I am profoundly convinced of the importance of the changes which are taking place. No one is in a better position than I am to appreciate the benefits which our rule has conferred on India. I have served for thirty-five years as a member of the Indian Civil Service. My father and grandfather were members of that service before me for sixty years. My son is now employed in that service. It is my pride that I am, as it were, a hereditary member of the Administration, and I have never been deficient in respect and loyalty to the Government. A spirit of devotion to the people of the country is not inconsistent with, and has never obliterated, my sense of official duties. But while I am not slow to recognise the valuable qualities of our English rule, I am equally assured that the benefits we have conferred will never receive their due fulfilment unless we can raise ourselves above associations of the official groove, and prepare ourselves for the exercise of higher functions than those of mere administration. The Government has deliberately infused new life into the Indian nation, and must not shrink from the responsibilities which are involved in giving full effect to this policy. What these responsibilities are, and what our future line of policy should be, are subjects which I have deemed it right to place before the consideration of the public.

HENRY COTTON.

November 1906.

CONTENTS

NEW INDIA

OR

INDIA IN TRANSITION

INDIA'S POLITICAL PROBLEM

THE test of a nation is that its members, among all kinds of partial differences, do, in the main, work together as fellow-citizens, linked by common memories and associations and common objects. Neither race nor language nor religion nor geographical boundary nor subjection to a common government is sufficient in itself to constitute a nation. It is not every population which constitutes a nationality, and the nations of the world are populations united in a very special way and by very special forces. By this test let India be judged. It is a trite saying that there is no Indian Nation. But apply the touchstone, and it will be seen that that statement is no longer true, and that there is at the present moment a New India rising before our eyes, a nation in the real sense in actual formation, with common sentiments of interest and patriotism. India in transition is New India, and the political problem in India is the growth of an Indian Nation.

We have done more under our rule than was ever attempted by our predecessors to make a nationality possible. India is a vast assemblage of different races, divided into numberless castes, classes, and creeds. The British Government is a supreme power separate and distinct from all the units which acknowledge its sway. But unsympathetic as the subject races may be among themselves—and my experience is that we grossly exaggerate their want of sympathy—our Government is even more unsympathetic with all of them, and a probability therefore always exists that they will consent to merge their own minor differences and unite in their attitude towards the common head. An organisation only is wanted, around which the elements of a nationality may cluster.

We have ourselves established the basis of such an organisation. In accordance with a noble and liberal policy, we have extended to India the inestimable boon of education. It is education, and education according to English methods and on the lines of Western civilisation, that has served to unite the varying forces among the Indian populations. No other bond of unity was possible : the confusion of tongues was an insuperable obstacle. But now the English language is the channel through which the fire-worshippers of Bombay and the Baboos of Bengal, the Brahmins of Madras and the Mahrattas of Poona, the Pathans and Rajpoots of Upper India and the Dravidian races of the other extreme end of the peninsula, are able to meet on one common platform, and to give expression to their common interests and aspirations. At the same time the railways, the steamships, the post-office, and the telegraph have played their part in connecting the gap that used to keep the different provinces of India asunder.

The germ of a national organisation on the basis of English education has long existed, but it has sprung into its present vigour in very recent times. Its present development is due to causes intended to produce a very different effect. The Anglo-Indian agitation against Lord Ripon's government, of which we once heard so much, the protests which asserted that "the only people who have any right to India are the British," the whole attitude, in brief, of Englishmen in regard to Indian interests, have tended far more to advance the true cause of Indian unity than any action or legislation on the lines contemplated by that Viceroy could have accomplished. That humble measure known as the Ilbert Bill—which was designed to supplement Lord Macaulay's so-called "Black Act" of fifty years before, and to remove all distinctions of race in respect of criminal jurisdiction—if it had been allowed to pass without opposition, would have proved innocuous and comparatively ineffective in any direction. But the unreasonable clamour and rancour of its opponents and the unexpected success which attended their efforts gave rise to a counter-agitation of the most far-reaching character. Clamour was met by clamour, and a national agitation, published and disseminated by means of the English language, was carried on throughout the length and breadth of India. The very object was attained which the Anglo-Indian agitators, if they had been wise in their generation, would have spared no labour to prevent. The people of India were not slow to follow the example set to them by Englishmen : they have learnt their strength, the power of combination, the force of numbers ; and there has now been kindled in all the provinces of India a national movement which is destined to develop and increase until it receives its fulfilment in the systematic regeneration of the whole country.

The earliest evidence of a national organisation manifested itself in the extraordinary enthusiasm with which the natives of India, of all races and creeds, united to honour Lord Ripon on the occasion of his departure from India. Such demonstrations in honour of a retiring Viceroy are altogether a novel phenomenon. The homage that was tendered to Lord Ripon was never before offered to any foreign ruler. The spectacle of a whole nation stirred by one common impulse of gratitude was never before witnessed in Indian history. No demonstration could have been more characterised by both unanimity and spontaneity. No sign could show more clearly that the germ of a nationality had already sprung into life.

Lord Ripon left India a little more than twenty years ago, and the First Indian National Congress met in 1885, the year after his departure. The sources of their inspiration are, therefore, within the memory of men who are still young. The date of Lord Ripon's departure is the natal day of a New India; and if the national vitality flagged or seemed to flag for a brief moment after its birth, it has been galvanised into vigorous adolescence by recent events, and the movement now advances by leaps and bounds.

The outpouring of Indian aspiration and the unmistakable yearning for Indian nationality find their utterance through a newspaper press, now becoming a potent factor in Indian politics, and in the annual meetings of the Provincial and National Congresses.

The Indian press has grown in one generation, from struggling, obscure, and fitful efforts, into an organ of great power, criticising the measures of Government with remarkable independence and vigour, continually checking the abuses of executive authority, and permeating all classes of the community, who are animated by its energy, and proud of the ability and patriotism with which it is conducted.

The newspaper press in India is now recognised as a kind of constitutional opposition, and with the growth of this recognition its importance is assured. It has also acquired new strength from the reactionary tendencies of bureaucratic rule. Legislation designed to curtail the liberty of the press and speech; the crusade against so-called sedition; the attempt to abolish trial by jury; the forcible introduction of harsh plague regulations, subsequently withdrawn; the blows that have been dealt at local self-government, especially in Calcutta; the systematic discouragement of popular institutions; the deliberate encouragement of provincial segregation; the substitution of a system of nomination to Government service in the place of competitive examinations; the practical declaration of race disqualification for public offices; the hampering and fettering of unaided colleges and schools, and the general sinister drift in favour of officialising all branches of education; and, above all, the recent partition of Bengal, which was not only carried out in direct opposition to the wishes of the people, and in spite of their most vigorous protests, but was enforced with a degree of harshness and want of sympathy which are fortunately rare in the annals of Indian administration,—these and other measures have had their effect in inspiring the opposition with fresh life. This is always the result of reaction; and in every campaign of agitation, the power and influence of the Indian press have been augmented. The unanimity of this press is as marked as the increase of its influence. The same tone characterises its utterances in Calcutta, Madras, Bombay, Lahore, and Allahabad. The whole of its influence is in the direction of nationalisation. There is no doubt of its meaning, its character, or its destination. A single note is struck. In every large town in India newspapers are now published, identical in their spirit and in their common object, all aiming and converging at the formation of a single political ideal.

Side by side with the Indian press there is working the organisation known as the Indian National Congress. This organisation is avowedly national in its name and scope. The Provincial Congresses, which meet in every province for the discussion of provincial matters, unite together in a National Congress, which is held annually at a chosen centre, for the furtherance and discussion of national interests. A Congress consists of from five hundred to one thousand of the political leaders of all parts of India, comprising representatives of noble families, landowners, members of council, members of local boards and municipalities, honorary magistrates, fellows of universities, and professional men, such as engineers, bankers, merchants, shopkeepers, journalists, lawyers, doctors, priests, college professors, and others. The delegates at these Congresses are able to act in concert, and to declare, in no uncertain accents, the common public opinion of the multitudes of whom they are the mouthpiece. They are as representative in regard to religion as to rank and profession. Hindoos, Parsees, Christians, and Mahomedans have in turn presided. Their deliberations are characterised by acumen and moderation. I take it upon myself to say, as a watchful eye-witness from its birth, that the Indian National Congress has discharged its duties with exemplary fidelity, judgment, and moderation. If its members have not in any considerable measure succeeded in moulding the policy of Government, they have at least exercised an immense influence in developing the history of their country and the character of their countrymen. They have become a power in the land, and their voice peals like a trumpet-note from one end of India to the other. The principal items of the Congress propaganda at the present time constitute a practical programme displaying insight and sagacity, and covering most of the political and economic problems of the Indian Empire. The impressions recorded by an English gentleman who was a spectator of the eighteenth meeting of the Indian National Congress, held at Ahmedabad in December 1902, are well worthy of reproduction. Mr Swinny writes :—

The Congress I found extremely interesting. Anglo-Indians represent it as a place where men of no political weight meet for idle declamation. I attended every sitting, and found the proceedings moderate and business-like throughout. There were a few foolish speeches and many wise ones. Eloquence there was in plenty, and it was difficult to believe that the speakers were speaking in a tongue that was not their own. The great tent in which the meetings were held, capable of holding some six thousand persons, was packed to hear the President's speech, and glowed with the varied colours of the turbans worn. Every community was represented. Learned Pandits from the North sat beside graduates of the English universities. Hindoos from Madras met those of Sindh; Mahrattas, Bengalees, native Christians, Jew doctors, Parsees, Mahomedan traders fresh from South Africa, all were there. The resolutions had a wide range. The economic situation, the threatened increase of military expenditure, the revenue from salt, and the Report of the Universities Commission —for India, too, has her education question—were among the subjects dealt with. But in reality the speeches and the resolutions were not the whole or even the greater part of the business. The Congress is the meeting-place of the political leaders of all parts of India. By it they have become able to work in concert. Through it a common public opinion has become possible. This is a result which no failure in their projects and no neglect of their advice can nullify.

As President of the Indian National Congress held at Bombay in December 1904, I can confirm these impressions. It is impossible to conceive of a more stirring spectacle than the beautiful city of Bombay presented on that occasion. The crowd in the public streets and in every balcony and window defied description. Traffic was suspended. The occupants of the tramcars, on their way to business, stood up to cheer. High and low, beggarmen and millionaires, joined in the procession. There never was a demonstration, since the departure of Lord Ripon twenty years before, to which the designation of 'national' could be more appropriately applied.

I have incidentally alluded to the partition of Bengal. Its wide-reaching influence on the national movement of the country calls for further treatment. It is not necessary to discuss the details of the measure, or the administrative reasons put forward in its justification. The scheme of partition naturally commended itself to the members of the Government services, who saw before them the attractive vista of additional offices and emoluments. But it was repugnant in the last degree to the inhabitants of the country, in whom there is a sense of patriotic pride in their province, their ancestry, and their future. The division of their people into two arbitrary sections gave a profound shock to the Bengalee race. But it did more than this. The sinister object of the measure was to shatter the unity and to disintegrate the feelings of solidarity which are established in the province. It was no administrative reason that lay at the root of this scheme. It was part and parcel of Lord Curzon's policy to enfeeble the growing power and destroy the political tendencies of a patriotic spirit. Bengalees are the leaders of political agitation in modern India. With all their faults, they are the principal section of the community which has inspired the future hope and destiny of their country. The consciousness and conviction that the partition was designed to weaken Bengalee influence induced the popular irritation on the subject. The measure was carried through against the will of the people, and in spite of their protests. They held innumerable public meetings and demonstrations; their local press was unanimous; they made every variety of representation by mail and cable; they exhausted the resources of constitutional agitation. At last they fell back on new methods, which resulted in the organisation of a *Swadeshi* or patriotic movement, the object of which is to encourage national manufactures and industries, and to prevent by every legitimate means the importation and consumption of foreign goods. This movement derives its origin and vitality from the unrest occasioned by the attempt to dissolve the ties of national unity. It is intensely national in character, and is the most practical and visible form in which the national tendencies of the country find their present expression.

New impulses also are springing up on every side and striking the chord of national life. The people of India are not blind to signs which all who run may read. Gleams of hope are reflected from the gradual solution of the Irish question, and the oft-repeated acknowledgment that Ireland must be governed in accordance with the wishes of her people. The progress of freedom's battle in Russia is eagerly watched and noted. The Egyptian movement, with its strong national leanings, reacts on India. The Pan-Islamic agitation, the popular movement in Persia, and even so-called Ethiopianism in South Africa, are not without their effect. The marked activity of young China, the persistent clamour for restoration of sovereign rights, the abolition of privileges granted to foreigners under the Treaties, the determined attempt to obtain possession of important sources of revenue hitherto controlled by Europeans—the signs of what is undisguisedly a national and patriotic movement in that great Eastern country—are echoed with sympathetic and intelligent interest in India.

It does not fail to attract notice that while opinion in England is generally hostile to any national movement which may be deemed to affect its own interests—such as the agitation in China, in Egypt, or in South Africa, not to speak of Ireland—it is ardently sympathetic with the revolutionary and wholly national movements in Russia and Macedonia, and even in Persia, which do not conflict with British interests, and have been inspired by the principles of liberty-loving Englishmen and the example of England itself.

Above all, there is Japan. What an inspiration has been afforded by the character of these Eastern islanders! What an example have they not set to the East of the power of a patriotic spirit! That example is not lost on India. The force which has made Japan what she is, is an absorbing patriotism derived from and dependent on her national existence. It is based on collective action, which independence alone can give. An alien government, however well-intentioned, cannot accomplish during many generations what national government has done in the space of less than forty years. The tendency of an alien government is too often in the direction, not of progress, but of disruption and reaction. The conditions in India do not point to any early renaissance such as we have witnessed in Japan. But the changes taking place there are no less due to the rising patriotism of the people. India is bereft of its independence. But the people of India have caught fire from the patriotic instincts which are animating the world around them, and a nascent nationalism is the magnet which holds together the solvent influences let loose on a community which has hitherto never felt their sway.

The growth of this national spirit marks the revolution to which India has been subjected in its political aspect. It proceeds hand in hand with the social and moral revolution, and is due to the same initial cause. But whereas in the one case it is not in the power of the authorities to exercise a beneficial interference, in the other it is not only within their power, but it is incumbent on them to act in co-operation with the people in furthering the changes already commenced. The danger is that by too tardy an acknowledgment of these changes we may drive the educated classes to force their opportunity before the country is ripe for such a consummation. At times of crisis, differences settle themselves roughly ; and those who have not advanced beyond the transition period will always be apt to be borne away by the violence of the stream. At such a moment true statesmanship will be evinced not only by care and caution, but also by wise encouragement.

Unfortunately such statesmanship is rare, and we are already confronted with this danger. The unsympathetic response which has been made to popular demands and the policy of reaction deliberately pursued in late years are the causes of that discontent and unrest, and impatience of the British connection with the country, which is the most ominous cloud upon the horizon of Indian politics. There is now a party of Indian nationalists who despair of constitutional agitation, and openly advocate the establishment of an absolutely free and independent form of national government in India. Their aim is to sever the connection between India and England altogether and at the shortest notice. Their object is to propagate a violent anti-British agitation, and, by any means in their power, to make British rule impossible in India. These men are a shadow of danger which casts itself over the future. Their attitude is the sign of an anarchical element in the continuity of India's political progress. A few years ago there was no possibility of the rise of such a party, which has sprung into life as a consequence of a policy which, while concentrating itself in perfecting details of administration, has proceeded in complete disregard of the wishes and feelings of the people affected. New difficulties, therefore, have arisen. But the members of this party are in a minority at present. Their powers are increasing, but they are not yet in the position of popular leaders. The recognised leaders of Indian thought and the original pioneers of the national movement are still unaffected by any symptoms of alienation from the British Government. They are men of moderate views, who exercise a healthy and restraining influence on the attitude of the extremists. Their ideal is not separation from Great Britain, or independence from the general control which they recognise must always be exercised over colonies and dependencies. They desire to obtain self-government and the detailed management of their own affairs. Their ideal is that India may ultimately be placed in a position corresponding to that of the self-governing colonies of the Empire. That is the ideal which they hold before them, knowing well that it can only be realised gradually and cautiously, and as the result of time and experience.

The heart of the Indian people is true to

England. In eloquent language Lord Curzon[1] once appealed to the citizens of Bombay: "I pray the native community in India to believe in the good faith and high honour and in the upright purpose of my countrymen." In these words he struck a glowing note. The people of India do believe in the good faith, honour, and integrity of Englishmen. They are grateful for the education with which they have been endowed; grateful for the liberties they enjoy; and grateful for their immunity from civil war and foreign invasion. But their gratitude is tempered by a feeling that the pledges held out to them by Her late Gracious Majesty Queen Victoria and by men in exalted positions have not been fulfilled. Their faith has been shaken, and a sense of disappointment, rapidly rising into bitterness, has been kindled amongst them. It is because their claims have been disregarded, their prayers rejected, and the co-operation of their leaders has been spurned, that the present difficulties have arisen.

There is now a change in the policy of the Indian Government. The existence of a Liberal Administration in England compels the adoption of liberal and sympathetic principles in dealing with Indian questions on the spot. The prac-

[1] On 9th December 1904.

tical difficulty is the impatience of the extreme section of the community. But this difficulty may easily be overcome if the members of the Government of India associate with themselves the leaders of Indian thought. Those leaders possess immense power and influence; and if the Government act with them and through them, and not against them, the disturbing tendencies of the extreme party will speedily subside.

There is no danger in this course. The leaders of the Indian movement are subject to the pressure of the enthusiasm of their followers. But they are not yet borne away by it. The formation of an extreme left among their own party is as embarrassing to them as it is to the Government. Their faith in British rule is firm and strong, their political instincts are abhorrent to any rupture with the past. They know that British rule in its present form cannot continue, but they know also that the connection between India and England will never be snapped. They know that the English language, while it is the means of enabling the different populations of India to attain unity, binds them also to Great Britain. It is from England that all the ideas of Western thought which are revolutionising the country have sprung; the language of Shakespeare and Milton has become the common language of India ; the future of India is linked with that of England, and it is to England that India must always look for guidance, assistance, and protection in her need.

Statesmanship consists in foreseeing, and we are all of us the better for the exercise of forethought. It is well, therefore, to familiarise ourselves with the conception which the realisation of a national spirit in India involves. It was the dream of John Bright, and he indulged in no mere mystic prophecy when he foresaw that India would fulfil her ultimate destinies by a process of evolution, out of which she would emerge, not through force or violence as an independent State, or torn from us or abandoned to England's enemies, but as a federated portion of the dominion of the great British Empire. As philosophic observers, we may see the future of India unfold itself before us. As practical statesmen, we may assist and encourage its evolution. We may assert with confidence that India will no more break from its connection with England than it will from the Hindoo or Mahomedan periods of its history. We may anticipate a time when the existence of healthy relations will be guaranteed by the establishment of a federation of free and separate States, placed on a fraternal footing with our great self-governing colonies, each with its now local autonomy and independence, under the immediate supremacy of England. And we may venture to look for the basis of internal order to the recognition of that organisation which from time immemorial has existed in India—a patrician aristocracy of indigenous growth, trained by past associations to control and lead the lower orders of the people.

This is the forecast of a future, dim and distant though it be, the gradual attainment of which it is the privilege of Government to regulate. It is a conception which gathers as it grows, and insensibly attracts into the political evolution all other great problems of economic and social reform. It demands from our Indian Government a capacity for reconstruction, for guidance and sympathy during a period of transition, for energy and action when it is necessary to advance, for masterly inactivity and watchful repose when it is more necessary to look to the encouragement of spontaneous development. It calls for the qualities of statesmanship rather than of administrative ability. There is no country more easy to administer than India, where the people are so law-abiding and so amenable to authority. It is easy to administer uprightly the affairs of a docile and subject people; it is easy, with the power of British bayonets at our back, to coerce refractory rajahs, and to settle by secret diplomacy the conflicting interests of native States ; it is easy to lead our victorious armies among imperfectly armed and semi-savage nationalities, to annex provinces, and by despotic rule evolve order out of chaos. It is a sublimer function of imperial dominion to unite the varying races under our sway into one empire, "broad-based upon the people's will" ; to fan the glowing embers of their national existence ; to afford scope to their patriotic aspirations, and to wait upon, foster, and protect the peaceful organisation of their political federation and autonomous independence as the ultimate basis of relationship between the two countries.

INDIAN OPINION AND ASPIRATIONS

NOTHING is more difficult than for an Englishman to probe the real meaning of Indian opinion, or to gauge the true character of Indian sentiments towards our rule. Obstacles of colour, of physique, of race, of religion, of language, of prejudice, present themselves at every turn to frustrate any real intimacy with the inhabitants of the country. It is very rarely that Indians will be found to express themselves with openness to a European. Were there no other reason, the peculiar official relationship would explain this. But, independently of any official relations, the attitude of Englishmen to Indians is not of a character to inspire confidence. Englishmen never know them in their homes. Indian gentlemen are therefore naturally exclusive and reserved. The longer we have occupied India, the less almost do we seem to know of the life of the people. The tendency, instead of being towards intercommunion, is rather in the direction of increased divergence.

We derive, moreover, the most false impressions of Indian thought from the Indians with whom we do come in contact. Those whom we ordinarily meet are either officials or else gentlemen of property and position, with whom it is a traditional duty to pay their respects to those in authority over them. They are men of rank and dignity, and are therefore entitled to honourable consideration, but they are not the mouthpiece of the people. Their conversation is not the echo of popular views and sentiments. Their voice strikes no responsive chord among the educated classes. Still less are those Indians in any degree representative whose highest pleasure it appears to be to fawn upon and flatter the members of the ruling race. There is no more satisfactory token of the higher standard of thought which has accompanied English education than the spirit of disapprobation with which these men are regarded by the stronger and more restless and independent among their fellow-countrymen. There are wealthy Indian gentlemen who court the company of officials, and do not scruple to dispose of their Indian guests with scanty ceremony, while they reserve the grandest display, the richest luxuries, and the choicest amusements for the delectation of their European guests. At such entertainments, where Viceroys have been spectators, I have seen caricatures of Indian life presented on the stage for the amusement of Europeans. These caricatures are amusing, no doubt, but for the Englishmen who behold them they only afford material for satire, and for increasing the contempt with which the natives are already regarded. The spirit of self-abasement which degrades itself to giving such an entertainment excites indignation in nobler minds; and yet English officials, from the Viceroy downwards, who are held to honour such spectacles by their presence, believe that by so doing they ingratiate themselves with the Indian community, and bridge the gulf between the races. Vain delusion! They foster the pushing, the cringing, the slavish instinct among the natives, which needs no encouragement.

The really best men among the natives of India, who influence opinion and lead society not less by their intellectual accomplishments than in virtue of the moral qualities of honesty and independence, are naturally of a more retiring disposition and somewhat proud. They do not care to make the acquaintance of Government officials if they can help it, and they do not thrust themselves on the Government. They are not to be found on railway platforms to receive officials or bid them good-bye; they do not attend meetings with the sole object of picking up influential acquaintances. They do not dedicate books to officials, organise ovations for them, or seek to perpetuate their names by public buildings, roads, and so forth. Wise in their own reticence, dignified in their self-respect, the true leaders of Indian opinion pursue their own course with as little communication with Europeans as is consistent with the exercise of their full influence. Englishmen hear little of them, and the Government, too often, knows them not; but their names are household words among the homes of the people.

The public opinion of India is moulded in the metropolis, and takes its tone almost entirely from the educated community which centres in the chief towns. Except in regard to their own local affairs, the masses of the people are indifferent, not as to the manner in which, but as to the hands by which, the powers of government are exercised over them. They look to their educated countrymen for guidance. Calcutta is now more to Bengal than Paris is to France. Madras and Bombay are no less forward than Calcutta in the dissemination of political thought and action. No one can pretend to possess any knowledge of Indian feeling who does not keep his finger on the pulse of opinion in the Presidency towns. There is a growing unanimity of opinion throughout India, based on the increased solidarity of Indian thought and the spread of English education. The people of India cannot but act and think as that section of the community which monopolises the knowledge of politics and administration may instruct them.

The educated classes are the voice and brain of the country. The educated followers of Islam, although they are comparatively few in number, are animated by the zeal and vigour and austerity which have always characterised the religious history of their race. The highly-trained, wealthy, and energetic Zoroastrians of Bombay have pushed themselves to the front in every department of life in that Presidency, and mould its destinies alike in commerce and intellectual pursuits. The brilliant and patriotic Mahrattas, exulting in their past and in the glory of their ancestors, unite with the Parsees in all their political aspirations, and exercise a wider influence by virtue of the living Hindooism which lies at the heart of their national existence. The Brahmins of Madras, with their keen and subtle intelligence, and a knowledge and mastery of the English language unsurpassed, have stirred a wave of thought which has swelled into every corner of Southern India. The Baboos of Bengal have done even more. They now rule public opinion from Peshawar to Chittagong; and although the natives of North-Western India are immeasurably behind those of Bengal in education and in their sense of political independence, they are gradually becoming as amenable as their brethren of the lower provinces to intellectual control and guidance. A few short years ago and there was no trace of this; the idea of any Bengalee influence in the Punjab would have been a conception incredible to Lord Lawrence, to a Montgomery or a Macleod; yet I remember the tour of a Bengalee lecturer, lecturing in English in Upper India, assuming the character of a triumphal progress; and at the present moment the name of Surendro Nath Banerjea excites as much enthusiasm among the rising generation of Mooltan as in Dacca.

In former times the masses in India, so far as they were represented at all, depended on the English officials of the country for support. Such representation was obviously of the most imperfect description, but it existed to some extent, and served at least to protect the people from oppression at the hands of the non-official or 'interloper' European element. The early effects of English education did not disturb this state of things; on the contrary, the tendency among the educated natives, who were imbued with Western ideas, was rather to hold themselves aloof from the people. They were highly educated in comparison with the masses, and all their new associations induced them to separate from their own countrymen. But now their attitude is changed. The educated Indians, as they increase in number, become more and more the rivals of Englishmen, and especially of the official class, who stand between them and the prizes of their ambition. As their numbers increase they become less isolated among themselves, and fall back more and more on the community to which they belong. One of the healthiest impulses which can be traced in Hindoo society is the corresponding change which has come over the masses of the people, who have now learnt to transfer their allegiance to the educated classes as their natural and best representatives.

I cannot too strongly protest against the fashion of deriding the Indian movement as a mere schoolboy agitation. It is untrue that the leaders of Indian thought are comparatively young, or that their followers are to a large extent mere students of our colleges. The movement has become national in its character, and is representative of educated Indian opinion in all parts of the country. But I am not blind to the powerful influence that is exercised by the enthusiasm of the rising generation. I do not forget that the student class has been largely instrumental in the formation of public opinion in Europe, and I am not surprised that the students in India should be active in the dissemination of opinion in that country. The vitality of the movement and the surest guarantee of its persistence are to be found in the fact that it is taken up by those who have all the vigour and energy of youth. No wise statesman in any country, and least of all in India, where education, which has roused all this movement, is still young, and New India, to which the movement has given birth, is still in its infancy, would venture to despise the public opinion which emanates from youthful agitators and patriots. And yet we have witnessed a deliberate attempt to dragoon loyalty into the schools of Eastern Bengal. There could be no more fatuous folly than the measures that were adopted to repress patriotic and national manifestations by the cruel and indiscriminate persecution of schoolboys. It was the sowing of the dragon's teeth. For it is these striplings of the present generation who are the fathers of the next.

The attitude of Anglo-Indians is an indication of the unsympathetic relations which exist between the two races. For the most part it is an attitude of complete indifference. Englishmen in India are blind to the real and obvious meaning of the great changes which are taking place before their eyes. They know not the machinery which works the change, and they see not the change itself. They live and behave, as far as possible, as though they were not in India at all. I am glad to acknowledge that there are many honourable exceptions, but, speaking generally, there is need of little qualification. The mercantile community, immersed in its own affairs, possesses neither the leisure nor the inclination to associate with the educated class of natives any further than may be necessary for the transaction of business. Its members acquire the usual prejudice against 'natives,' which seems almost inseparable from our position in the East, but they gain with it no knowledge whatsoever of Indian affairs or of the Indian character. Their estimate is nothing more than a traditional prejudice inherited from a preceding generation, and never put to the test of experience. The officers of the army are, with a few exceptions, wholly ignorant of all classes of the people, except the soldiers under their immediate command. The members of the Civil Service and the other civilian subordinates of Government enjoy, no doubt, a wider perception of the social and political revolution, but for the most part their experience is confined to outlying tracts and provincial towns, and the changes effected come, therefore, comparatively little under their observation. They are deceived also by the glamour of their position, and by the sycophancy with which they are usually pursued by individuals whose first object is to stand well with those in power. They are predisposed by all their associations, interests, and antecedents to deny the possibility of any radical change. Even when they are compelled to acknowledge the existence of any considerable popular movement, they will generally be found to depreciate its significance. Lastly, it must be added that the Government itself is not in a position to grasp the true meaning of the situation. Far removed in the serene Himalayan heights, it is not susceptible to the influences to which it would be subjected in the great capitals; and it labours under this disadvantage, that it is surrounded by advisers whose experience has been gained elsewhere than in the metropolis, and otherwise than by association with the real leaders of Indian thought.

He would be a bold man who would unhesitatingly affirm that the people of India are friendly to the British Government. If outward manifestations are of any avail, there ought to be no doubt of the loyalty of the great chiefs who from time to time have offered to place, and actually have placed, their armies at the disposal of Government, who have visited England to testify their allegiance to their Sovereign, and have taken their part in the pomp and ceremony of the Delhi Durbar, and have there rendered their personal and humble obeisance to the representative of the Crown ; of the Indian press and of the Indian National Congress, who have always been unanimous in their protestations of loyalty ; and of the popular leaders who have set on foot a movement for the enlistment of Indian volunteers who desire to serve shoulder to shoulder with Englishmen in the defence of their country. But I must caution my readers not to be carried away unduly by these manifestations. Their meaning is different if we consider the different classes from which they come.

It would perhaps be ungenerous to probe too narrowly the dependent position and consequent involuntary action of the feudatory chiefs. They are powerless to protect themselves. There is no judicial authority to which they can appeal. There is no public opinion to watch their interests. Technically independent under the suzerainty of the Empire, they are practically held in complete subjection. Their rank and honours depend on the pleasure of a British Resident at their Court, and on the secret and irresponsible mandates of a Foreign Office at Simla. It is impossible to imagine a more sensitive body than our Indian feudatories. They are consumed by petty jealousies among themselves, by questions of precedence, of salutes, of the strength of their armies. The example of one chief is infectious, the others cannot be outdone, and thus they vie with one another in their enthusiastic receptions of the Viceroy on his occasional visits, and in the display of those barbaric attributes of loyalty which are the surest passport for recognition and favour from the Government. They know that the annexation policy of Lord Dalhousie is still cherished among the Indian services, and that the proposal is unceasingly made that their troops should be disbanded. But the maintenance of their armies is a point of honour vital to their integrity as independent chiefs. It was a self-preserving instinct, rather than any sentiment of loyalty, which placed their soldiers at the disposal of the paramount power, and thereby warded off the ignominy of disbandment at any future time. There was little spontaneity; but they risked and could have risked nothing by their action, and have gained much. They have won the reputation of loyalty.

I do not imply by these remarks that there are not powerful and loyal princes whose attachment and devotion to the Crown is heartfelt and sincere. I have no doubt that the martial spirit, which our present policy has done much to encourage, tends unmistakably to kindle in the younger chiefs a glow of ambition and pride in the Empire in which they play their part. I am convinced that a Russian conquest would be as abhorrent to the native princes of India as it undoubtedly would be to the people generally; but I do say that the real motive power for the outward and visible signs of loyalty which have been so effusively displayed of late is due far less to their love or admiration for the British Government than to the peculiar helplessness of their position, and in no small measure to a keen perception of political opportunity, from which they have not failed to score a diplomatic advantage.

If the ruling princes of India are to be inspired with a real sense of loyalty, it can only be done by humouring and conciliating them, and taking every care not to offend their susceptibilities or lower their prestige. Their rule may not be an ideal one, but it is far more humane, sympathetic, and popular than we are apt to think. It is not a wise policy to be always lecturing them and posing as their pedagogue in public. They do not require to be reminded of the might and majesty of the suzerain power ; that reminder is always at their side in the Agent to the Governor-General or the Resident. The policy of the Delhi Durbar in respect of these great feudatories was the subject of common discussion at the Durbar itself and in the columns of the newspaper press throughout India. It was said that they were humiliated by the loss of their prestige and the public parade of their subject position. If the King had been present in person, or if the Duke of Connaught had been deputed to preside, there would have been neither reluctance felt nor humiliation. But the idea of a subject of the Crown receiving their obeisance and their homage, while the brother of the King was forced into the background, and the plebeian spectators held up their heads and clapped their hands and looked on as if they were the occupants of a seat in a circus or theatre, was as unintelligible to them as it was degrading and distasteful. In this manner was it proclaimed to the world that they were no longer independent princes in alliance with His Majesty, but mere vassals of the Empire. We are told that their degradation was deeply felt by them ; and it is hardly to be supposed that their loyalty could have been stimulated by their inclusion in Lord Curzon's triumph after the fashion in which the captives of old accentuated the power of Rome by marching behind the chariot of the victorious consul.

It is not agreeable to our imperial vanity to acknowledge that the attitude of the Indian princes—their loyalty and their homage—is not primarily animated by spontaneous and unselfish motives complimentary to our rule ; but it is better to recognise the truth, and avoid thereby the grave political blunder into which we should otherwise fall.

Similarly, it is well that we should realise in its full measure the undercurrent of bitterness and discontent which so widely prevails among the members of the educated and English-speaking community, and not attach undue importance to the newspaper utterances and other expressions of loyalty of which so much has been made. These men also are prudent in their generation. I do not doubt the genuineness of their manifestations. They are based upon a fervent and wise desire to maintain the material basis of existing order in its integrity, to avoid premature change, and to preserve the *status quo* until modifications can be introduced with greater advantage. The horror of Russian invasion is a sentiment universal among all classes. The people of India do not like the English dominion, but they do not wish to see a change of masters. The educated classes like the dominion of England least of all; but the educated classes most of all desire that there may be no sudden change. They fear lest a worse thing should befall them. They know that the abolition of English dominion would be accompanied by incalculable disaster. They know that if we were voluntarily to retire from India, without guarantee of any kind for peace or order, they would instantly be subjugated by fierce and unlettered warriors. They know perfectly well that if the English were driven out of India by the Russians, an imperial Russian

Government would prove less disinterested and philanthropic than an imperial British Government. They know at least that if the Russians were to come to India, all the advantages which they have so laboriously acquired through English education would be lost. Their knowledge of Russian administration and Russian policy is very imperfect ; and being tainted in every particular by English prejudices, which they have derived from their English education, their dislike and dread of Russia is (with better reason, no doubt) even greater than that of Anglo-Indians, whose language and style in speaking of Russia they imitate. I apprehend, therefore, that the expression of their sentiments against Russia, and of their desire to support and even fight for England in her need, is undoubtedly genuine. But it is somewhat exaggerated also. Many of the Indian newspapers, with shrewd instinct, do not fail to perceive the advantage of writing up Indian loyalty, and of thereby vindicating a claim to greater confidence and to a larger share in the administration. It is impossible to admit the loyalty and deny the claim. If the Government will take no higher grounds, it will perhaps concede something to Indian aspirations in consideration of the loyalty of its Indian subjects.

The truth, however, of all the manifestations on the part of the educated Indian community is, as I have already indicated, that they are evidence, not of the zeal of the natives of India in support of our Government, but of their anxiety that that Government may not be replaced by a worse one. They are signs neither of loyalty nor disloyalty. The use of such words as 'loyalty' and 'disloyalty' is meaningless when applied to the natives of a dependency like India. They are loyal in that they appreciate the advantages of British rule, and are grateful to the British Government for the benefits which have been conferred on them.[1] If this constitutes loyalty, they are loyal. They do not demand that the British ascendency should be subverted. But they are embittered, deeply embittered, at their exclusion from power, at the deliberate neglect of assurances in their favour solemnly made and repeatedly renewed, at the

[1] This feeling has been well expressed by a native writer in the columns of the *Indian Nation*, a paper ably conducted and most appropriately designated :—"An enlightened administration of justice, especially in criminal cases, religious toleration, liberty of the press, liberty of holding meetings and petitioning—these are rights which we in this country have so easily acquired that we are in danger of undervaluing them. We have secured by a few strokes of the pen of beneficent legislators, advantages which Englishmen have had in their own country to buy with their blood."

contemptuous manner in which they are treated by Europeans, and at the insolence with which their legitimate aspirations are spurned and set aside. If it is disloyalty to attempt to wring concessions from the Government by all fair means within their power, they are disloyal. If it is disloyalty, when excluded from office themselves, to watch and censure, often in no measured terms, the abuses of the authority exercised over them by Englishmen, they are disloyal. In the formation of public opinion they place themselves in opposition to the ruling race, and, in vindication of their own rights, criticise freely the policy of their governors and the action of the executive and judicial officers of Government. If this constitutes disloyalty, then they are disloyal. But they are not disloyal if disloyalty consists in the feeling that they would wish to see the English Government driven from India. That is not the feeling of the educated classes, and it is not the feeling of the nation. They tolerate the existence of our Government as an irrevocable necessity, which has done immense service to them in the past, but which they are determined to modify until it adapts itself to changes which, under its own impulse, have come into existence outside its constitution. They claim that the Government should repose confidence in them, and not shrink from raising them to the highest posts in civil and military life. They demand real, not nominal, equality, a voice in the government of their own country, and a career in the public service.

In this connection I am glad to subjoin the following quotation from the *Times* special article on Indian affairs, of the 29th July 1906, as indicating the growth of opinion on this point in England :—"We have thrown open to the educated classes a literature, every page of which is full of the praise of liberty and patriotism. To secure the circulation of the ideas which our literature begets, we have introduced the printing press and the daily newspaper, and conceded full liberty of speech and of the press. And lest the people should fail to catch the teachings of the facts before their eyes, we have on two memorable occasions gone out of our way to declare that no Indian should, by reason only of his religion, place of birth, descent, or colour, be precluded from holding any office in the Government for which he is qualified. The peoples of India would have been less than human had they not taken these lessons to heart, had they not, after more than half a century of such teaching, begun to ask their rulers for a larger share in the government of their country."

We have been turning out year by year and month by month from our universities and schools streams of men with the best education that the English Government could give them. We have been throwing open to them English ideas and English thoughts, and have awakened in their minds many an aspiration, and kindled in their hearts legitimate ambition. Is it possible to turn round on these men and say to them—we will not give you any opening for these aspirations with which we have inspired you ; we will not afford you any means for the satisfaction of that ambition which we have created? Right well might Lord Ripon declare[1] that to make such an answer seemed to him the height of political folly. Right well, too, was it for him to quote the words of Macaulay in the House of Commons, when he said : "Are we to keep these men submissive? or do we think we can give them knowledge without awakening ambition? or do we mean to awake ambition and provide it with no legitimate vent? Who will answer any one of these questions in the affirmative? Yet one of them

[1] Speech of Lord Ripon at the banquet given to him at the Leeds Liberal Club in 1885.

must be answered in the affirmative by every person who maintains that we ought permanently to exclude the people of India from high office. I have no fears. The path of duty is plainly before us, and it is also the path of wisdom, of national prosperity, and of honour."

I can indeed conceive no more ignoble or unworthy policy than that a great power like England should avowedly continue to govern the Indian people with the deliberate intention of holding them in perpetual subjection, and with a set purpose of preventing their advance to freedom. This was the policy enunciated by Lord Ellenborough in his evidence before Parliament in 1853. It was re-echoed by the whole Anglo-Indian community in their opposition to Lord Ripon in 1883. It still reverberates in every nook and corner of the Anglo-Indian press and of Anglo-Indian society. Nothing is more deplorable than the unwillingness of the English community in India to recognise the signs of the times, and their inability to review a position which the march of events has rendered no longer tenable. The immediate outlook, therefore, is not a bright one. There are brilliant exceptions. But Anglo-Indians, as a body, have shown themselves incapable of appreciating the new political forces which education and Western civilisation have brought into prominence. Their bitterness of dislike towards the members of the subject races has been aggravated by this incapacity. No help, therefore, is to be expected from them. Even the great majority of the officials employed under Government are in complete accord with non-officials in this respect, and are as directly opposed as non-officials can be to giving effect to a policy of general sympathy and encouragement of all national and popular aspirations.

THE INCREASED BITTERNESS OF RACE FEELING

THE remarks contained in the previous chapter lead me to further reflections regarding the existing relations between Englishmen and the natives of India. The subject is a painful one, but I cannot avoid it in these pages. I cannot say that the relations have ever been of a healthy character. Never at any time was there any real sympathy between the races, any sign of intercommunion, or of blending the two nations into one. There has always been a sense of dislike. Sir Walter Scott expresses the prevailing sentiment of race feeling, fostered by religious prejudice, very neatly in *St Ronan's Well*, by the mouth of Captain MacTurk, where he says: "Py Cot! and I can tell you, sir! . . . . Cot tamn! Compare my own self with a parcel of black heathen bodies and natives that never were in the inner side of a kirk whilst they lived, but go about worshipping stocks and stones, and swinging themselves upon bamboos, like peasts, as they are!" Even so great a man as Lord Macaulay, with his liberal ideas, was not free from violent anti-native prejudice; and his description of the Bengalee character, which has tended to influence injuriously the attitude of thousands towards the Bengalee race, may be said to undoubtedly reflect the feeling of his contemporaries. When such sentiments were openly expressed, the relations cannot have been healthy. But generally speaking, I gather that in olden times the feeling of the ruling race towards the subject people was characterised by an absence of that bitterness which is now its most marked feature. The tone of feeling was rather one of lordly superiority and of contemptuous indifference.

This is the inherent attitude of Englishmen in regard to all coloured races. It would be too much to affirm that it is their attitude in regard to all other races than their own; but in respect of the so-called backward races there can be no doubt. Mr Bryce[1] has gone so far as to say: "It needs something more than the virtue of a philosopher, it needs the tenderness of a saint, to preserve the same courtesy and respect

[1] Romanes Lecture delivered at Oxford in 1902.

towards the members of a backward race as are naturally extended to equals." I resent this conclusion as an unworthy reflection on our higher culture and on the nobler instincts of our nature ; but it is an indication of frailty which finds expression in all quarters of the globe, and is a melancholy evidence of unwholesome racial conditions which are as permanent in their type and normal in operation as they are ineradicable in their tendency to prevent assimilation between the denizens of the East and West. There is a prejudice against a dark skin. "I cannot stand these natives: I think they are such rank outsiders." Such is the curious emanation of opinion which a stranger within the gates does not hesitate to apply to the people of the country.

The average Anglo-Indian view of the difficulties of inter-racial intercourse in India was not inadequately expressed by Sir Lepel Griffin, at a meeting of the East Indian Association in London, when he said that "so long as the Hindoo would not dine with an Englishman, so long as the Indian refused to bring his ladies into the common society, the difficulty of social intercourse between East and West would remain. The root of the matter is caste and race differences." This is a favourable statement of the Anglo-Indian view of the case ; but no view could be more superficial. The Hindoo does not dine with the Mussulman or with the Indian Christian, or with the Hindoo who has visited Europe ; the different Hindoo castes do not dine together, nor can they intermarry with one another ; and yet the relations between them are not strained, and the caste system has never stood in the way of social intercourse between the different races and castes of India. The social relations between Hindoos and Mahomedans are of the most cordial character ; and yet Hindoo and Mahomedan ladies never appear in society, and are strangers to those social amenities in which their male relations take part. The Mogul conquerors mixed freely and intimately with Hindoos, and racial differences have never interfered with the social relations of their descendants. The Parsees are another people who find no difficulty in establishing intimate relations and friendship with the old inhabitants of the country. There is, in fact, no race in India except the European which is marked by its social isolation from other classes of the community.

Again, if we regard the case from another aspect, we find that there are a considerable number of educated Indian gentlemen in India, many of whom have been to England and have associated on terms of equality with Englishmen: these gentlemen have no caste and are often willing to take their ladies into society, and yet there is no more social intercourse between them and Anglo-Indians than between Anglo-Indians and the rest of the Indian people. It does not matter whether natives of India live in English style or whether they do not, but they are not allowed admission into English society, or into Anglo-Indian clubs. What Anglo-Indian is there who cannot recall the scandals which have taken place in Government House when Indian gentlemen, albeit of the highest position, men whom in England we should be proud to meet, have been officially told off to take English ladies in to supper? An under secretary of my Government, a Cambridge graduate and a barrister-at-law of the Middle Temple, a gentleman of high attainments and marked amiability of character, was not allowed access to our station club. It would be easy to multiply such cases. It is narrated by Lieutenant-Colonel Graham in his *Life of Sir Syed Ahmed*, on the authority of the late Mr Justice Mahmood, that when that distinguished judge, during a visit to Madras, was taken by the then Chief Justice, Sir Charles Turner, to the Madras Club, a member promptly came up and told the Chief Justice, to Mr Mahmood's face, that "no native was allowed in the club," and both Sir Charles and Mr Justice Mahmood had at once to leave the club premises.

In the light of facts of this nature, it is impossible to believe in any theory that "the caste whims and prejudices of our Indian fellow-subjects stand in the way of friendship to an extent that renders all other difficulties altogether insignificant by comparison." Sitting at meals together may add to sociability, and ladies' society will give a charm to what may otherwise be lacking in friendly relations, but the "root of the matter" lies deeper than in caste and race differences: it is buried in the foundations and sunk in the framework of human weakness, deep in the prejudices of a ruling race, and inherent in the unsympathetic and arrogant attitude of white men in contact with a coloured people.

The warning which the late Marquis of Salisbury, when he was Secretary of State for India, as long ago as 1875, gave to the students at Cooper's Hill College is as true now as when it was uttered. "No system of government," he said, "can be permanently safe where there is a feeling of inferiority or of mortification affecting the relations between the governing and the governed. There is nothing I would more earnestly wish to impress upon all who leave this country for the purpose of governing India than that, if they choose to be so, they are the only enemies England has to fear. They are the persons who can, if they will, deal a blow of the deadliest character at the future rule of England." They are indeed the truest and most loyal servants of the British Government who exercise whatever influence they possess to soften asperities, to inspire confidence and respect, and to insist on moderation. The security of our Raj in India depends more on the existence of sympathy and good-will than on British bayonets, and those are the real friends of India whose successful administration is due to sympathy. They are the real enemies of the British Raj, and not its friends, who do but weaken our hold on the country by their unsympathetic treatment of its people. The warning of Lord Salisbury was a wise one. But he continued, with words of misplaced assurance, that he was convinced that all would take a better and higher view of their responsibility, and that as time went on the body of students who were turned out from England would go forth "feeling their position as missionaries of civilisation, and fully recognising the responsibility that lay upon them of drawing tighter the bonds between England and that splendid Empire with which it is our vast responsibility to deal." Noble words! but the spirit of optimism by which they are dictated is sadly at variance with the realities of experience. The danger to our rule remains with us, and far from diminishing, has increased with time and changing influences and the altered conditions under which our officials are now employed.

It were idle to deny that the sympathies of the two races are less kindly now than they were in the days of a past generation. Formerly English officials, notwithstanding their occasional sacrifice of self-respect, did succeed in some measure in identifying themselves with the people. Their devotion to India was not diverted into other channels. Their home became their adopted country. Now things are changed; their successors, regarding their functions as disagreeable and temporary, seize every opportunity to escape from them by frequent furloughs to Europe or by retiring as soon as possible. The Englishman in India has become less Indian and more English in his habits and feelings. It has been shrewdly said: "The Suez Canal has brought England and India closer together only to separate them the more." With stronger ties attaching them to England and increased facilities for visiting England, English officials grudge every hour of Indian service which keeps them from the West, where they have their real home. The feeling of impatience of their position, of anxious looking forward to the time when they can resign, is on the increase. Their sojourn in India bears more and more the character of an exile, and the exile sighs for home. Home yearnings, instinctively right in themselves, thus interrupt an active outflow of sympathy for their dark-skinned fellow-subjects.

The greater number of Englishmen who now find their way to India is also a reason for their greater alienation from the natives of the country. When they were few, isolated, and scattered, they were constrained by the force of circumstances to associate with the people. Now, in proportion as they are able to find companions among their own kinsfolk, they shrink from all avoidable communication with others, and their ignorance of the natives which results thereupon insensibly increases the bitterness of race feeling. Even the most narrow-minded members of the Anglo-Indian community do not dislike the Indians with whom they are intimately associated, but those only with whom they have little or no acquaintance.

Other influences are also in operation. The official mind is embittered by the increased worry of administering new taxes, and of yielding vastly more work under more arduous conditions. The abuse of power, which has always been dangerously stimulated by the peculiarities of our position, is now restrained by the expression of public criticism, which has, as it were, sprung suddenly into existence, and officials who have hitherto been practically irresponsible are irritated by the curtailment of their authority, and in many cases by its delegation to local boards and committees. It is a common complaint that officials nowadays have less consideration for the feelings of Indian gentlemen than in former times. Fresh from their studies, placed almost at once in a position calling for the exercise of a statesman's qualifications, with no knowledge of men or the habits of Indian social life, often without the smallest amount of tact for ruling or leading men, they surrender themselves habitually, when in the society of Indians, to an insolent demeanour of assumed superiority. A young magistrate who can maintain the dignity of his office with courtesy and conciliation is always respected ; and in such a case it will invariably be found that the administration of local interests by means of native co-operation is a marked success. But in the majority of cases—and unfortunately they are the majority—the proceedings of committees, benevolently designed by Government to bring together Europeans and Indians as much as possible for the management of business, are conducted throughout with hectoring language and in a bullying tone; and an Indian commissioner who ventures to evince any independence of character, or to oppose an opinion of the chairman, may consider himself lucky if he escapes without personal contumely or insult. Indian gentlemen go away silently; they rarely say what they feel; they would be horrified at anything like a scene, but they think and talk among themselves, and their feelings, we may be sure, are the reverse of respectful to our vaunted rule. At the same time we find in private life an almost universal use of irritating expressions in regard to Indians, which are not the less offensive when they proceed from persons who hold a responsible position, and have in other respects the outward seeming of English gentlemen. Among women, who are more rapidly demoralised than men, the abuse of "those horrid natives" is almost universal. Among men how often do we hear the term "nigger" applied, without any indication of anger or intentional contempt, but as though it were the proper designation of the people of the country! Even with those who are too well informed to use this term, the sentiment that prompts its use is not wholly set aside.

I cannot omit one feature of race prejudice which is rapidly developing into a source of embarrassment to the Administration. Assaults on natives by Europeans have always been of frequent occurrence, and it occasionally happens that they are attended with serious and sometimes fatal consequences. The trial of these cases, in which Englishmen are tried by English juries, too often results in a failure of justice not falling short of judicial scandal. During the past half-century there have been only two cases in which capital punishment has been inflicted on a European for the murder of a native, and in both these cases no stone was left unturned by Anglo-Indian agitation to obtain a reversal of the sentence. The character of such agitation affords one of the most painful manifestations of the bitterness of race feeling. If a tea-planter is charged with an outrageous assault upon a helpless coolie, he is tried by a jury of tea-planters, whose natural bias is in his favour;

but if, in any circumstances, such as by the interference of the High Court, or otherwise, a conviction should ensue, the whole volume of English opinion finds expression in denouncing the verdict, the Anglo-Indian newspapers add fuel to the flame and give free vent to this protest in their columns, public subscriptions are raised to pay the expenses of the culprit, and influentially signed memorials are addressed to the Government praying for his release. An Anglo-Indian Defence Association has been organised in Calcutta for the express purpose of defending such cases. A paragraph is published in the newspapers headed "A Planter in trouble," and forthwith all the flood-gates of passion and prejudice are let loose. Civilian magistrates even are not unaffected by race feeling. Their position is certainly a very difficult one, and it is impossible for them to be altogether uninfluenced by their environment and natural feelings towards their fellow-countrymen ; but this renders it all the more necessary for them to be on their guard against any display, or apparent display, of partiality. I am glad to acknowledge that in many conspicuous instances they discharge their invidious duties with exemplary firmness and courage ; but there is an undoubted tendency to inflict severe sentences when natives of India are concerned, and to impose light and sometimes inadequate punishment upon offenders of their own race.

It is impossible to read the record of these trials and not to feel that justice is not always well and duly administered between man and man. In the meantime a feeling of resentment and indignation is excited among the members of the Indian community, and the representative press on both sides runs riot in a violent and uncontrolled torrent of mutual recrimination. We are confronted by a problem of extreme administrative difficulty, in which the elements of race antagonism are vigorously reflected, and the most dangerous passions are roused. It is not easy to suggest a remedy, and for my part I do not know that any better or simpler scheme can be devised than the institution of special courts for the trial of cases in which Europeans are charged with the commission of serious offences. This remedy may not be wholly adequate, but it seems to afford the easiest solution.

I can unreservedly applaud Lord Curzon's policy in this matter. He spoke out plainly on the great question between man and man, and, although he quailed more than once before the storm of English race feeling, it is the merest justice to say that nothing more distinguished his administration of our Indian Empire than his overpowering detestation of injustice, and resolve to vindicate uprightness and punish wrongdoers.

The non-official community is naturally, instinctively, as it were, placed in a position of antagonism to the people of the soil. This fact is well brought out by John Stuart Mill,[1] who wrote many years ago in language which might have been uttered yesterday :—

> If there be a fact to which all experience testifies, it is that when a country holds another in subjection, the individuals of the ruling people who resort to the foreign country to make their fortunes are, of all others, those who most need to be held under powerful restraint. They are always one of the chief difficulties of the Government. Armed with the prestige and filled with the scornful overbearingness of the conquering nation, they have the feelings inspired by absolute power without its sense of responsibility. Among a people like that of India, the utmost efforts of the public authorities are not enough for the effectual protection of the weak against the strong; and of all the strong, European settlers are the strongest. Wherever the demoralising effect of the situation is not in a most remarkable degree

[1] Chapter xviii. of *Considerations on Representative Government*, which treats "of the government of dependencies by a free state."

corrected by the personal character of the individual, they think the people of the country mere dirt under their feet; it seems to them monstrous that any rights of the natives should stand in the way of their smallest pretensions; the simplest act of protection to the inhabitants against any act of power on their part, which they may consider useful to their commercial objects, they denounce and sincerely regard as an injury. So natural is their state of feeling in a situation like theirs, that even under the discouragement which it has hitherto met with from the ruling authorities it is impossible that more or less of the spirit should not perpetually break out. The Government itself, free from this spirit, is never able sufficiently to keep it down in the young and raw even of its own civil and military officers, over whom it has so much more control than over the independent residents.

It is a grave symptom that the official body in India has now succumbed as completely as the non-official to anti-native prejudices. I write in general terms, always remembering that there are many among my old colleagues and successors who rise above all prejudice and most honourably fulfil their obligations towards our Indian fellow-subjects; but, speaking generally, my statement calls for no further qualification. The time has passed away when non-official Englishmen formed one party in India and the Indians another, while the Government officials were charged with the function of protecting native interests; and instead thereof we now see a state of things in which the Indian community exists alone on the one side, while both classes of Englishmen, official as well as non-official, are united on the other. It is indeed a grave position to which we have drifted, for the change is complete and the tension acute.

In former times the civilian element in India was the self-constituted champion of native rights, and the people of the country always felt that the members of the Civil Service might be relied on to protect them from oppression at the hands of the English settlers. During the agitation which accompanied the passing of Macaulay's so-called Black Act—of which an instructive account will be found in Sir George Trevelyan's Life—when the whole non-official world was banded together to prevent what it conceived to be the injustice of allowing Indian judges to exercise civil jurisdiction over British-born subjects, the Civil Service as a body remained firm and supported the Government. During the indigo disturbances of the early sixties the civilians were the staunch friends and protectors of the cultivators against the indigo-planters, and incurred thereby an extraordinary amount of odium and obloquy. In those days it was the practice to blackball an official at the Bengal Club, whither men connected with indigo do most resort, merely because he was an official. There was little prospect then of the amalgamation of the two classes of Europeans, or of any identity of interests which would induce them to combine in a spirit of self-assertion against the natives.

The change is due partly to the enormously increased influence which the non-official European community now exercises. Their numbers have augmented, their interests in industries like jute and tea, coal and cotton have extended, and the Chambers of Commerce at the Presidency towns are now a power which is able to withstand the Government, and too often leads and dictates its policy. The position of officers scattered throughout a province, where the unofficial Europeans are the principal social force with which they are in contact, becomes one of increasing difficulty, and it is small wonder if they no longer display the independence and courage which were the attribute of their predecessors. The Government has grown too weak or is too demoralised to accord them its support. Few things are more remarkable in contemporary history in India than the sinister growth of this commercial influence over the executive Administration. Individual independence is now swept away by the pressure brought to bear upon it, and a John Peter Grant or an Ashley Eden who in these later days may venture to attempt to redress the wrongs of the weak and oppressed, does so at his peril.

The identification of interests of all classes of Europeans in India was Lord Curzon's consistent endeavour. To the tea-planters of Assam he said :[1]—"I look upon all Englishmen in this country as engaged in different branches of the same great undertaking. Here we are all fellow-countrymen, comrades, and friends. The fact that some of us earn our livelihood or discharge our duty by the work of administration, and others by cultivating the resources of the soil, does not differentiate us one from the other. These are merely the subdivisions of labour ; they are not distinctions of object or purpose or aim." And again, on another occasion, in addressing the mine-owners he declared :[2]—"My work lies in administration, yours in exploitation ; but both are aspects of the same question and of the same duty." There is no word of the obligation on English

[1] Speech at Cachar, November 1901.
[2] Speech at Burrakur, January 1903.

officials to devote themselves to the duty of championing the cause of their suffering fellow-subjects, or of protecting them from oppression ; no word of the duty of the strong to protect the weak. The warnings of John Stuart Mill are forgotten. The English in India must be either administrators or exploiters. The ideal of the far-off future is the perfection of the country by the twofold agency of British administration and British exploiting : all are alike engaged in the country's advancement. There is no sign of any appreciation of the capacities and claims of the Indian people, or any thought of the place they are to occupy after generations of foreign administration and exploitation. And yet the thought is one that must be always with us. The prosperity of a country has no meaning apart from that of the human beings who are born and dwell in it. To Englishmen the country may mean the soil of India, with all that is above and below it. To Indians it can only mean the people. This theory of identic British interests denotes, no doubt, the advancement of Englishmen, but it does not connote the welfare and happiness of the children of the soil. On the one side it has directly led to the formation of a solid phalanx of opinion in acute antagonism to Indian aspirations. On the other it has stirred the spirit of Indian opposition, and the bitterness of race feeling has been accentuated by the constant iteration of a policy in which the Indians have no part or share. They have learnt by experience that exploitation spells economic serfdom, and that British interests are hostile to their own.

There are other causes also at work set deeper in the very foundations of the structure upon which is based the fabric of India's evolution. This great change—the gradual amalgamation of opinion and interests among all classes of Englishmen, in contradistinction to the wishes and welfare of the Indian people—is due not only to the fulfilment of an economic policy, powerfully as that cause has operated, but even more largely to the universal tendencies upon which I have already so fully dwelt. The change was inevitable with the spread of English education. The Indian people have now found their voice, and their principal demand is, as might have been expected, for a larger share in the loaves and fishes of the Administration. A struggle is thereby generated with the official classes, and the sense of rivalry thus occasioned has created a more effective barrier between Indians and officials than that which has always been felt to exist between Indians and the non-official community. Both classes of Europeans are equally reluctant to admit the natives to equality, and the official class is especially aggrieved because Indians are invading preserves which have hitherto been free from any intruder.

The result of education has tended to equalise the races, and the nearer the equality the stronger the dislike. The more Anglicised an Indian is, the more he is disliked by Englishmen. The sense of jealousy becomes greater. Whatever may be professed, Englishmen are ready to encourage the natives who speak broken English more than those who speak good English, those who are subject to Hindoo prejudices more than those who have renounced them, and generally those who are far removed from English habits of thought and life more than those who have made a very close approach to them. They are more pleased with the backward Hindoo than with his advanced compatriot, because the former has made no attempt to attain equality with themselves.

This abhorrence of equality rankles in the mind of all Anglo-Indians, and especially of officials. It is the peculiarity of residence in the East to develop sentiments of intolerance and race superiority. It is painful to observe the habitual and almost universal exhibition of race insolence displayed by our fellow-countrymen as soon as they come in contact with a lower scale of civilisation. It may not need "the tenderness of a saint," but it is not the attribute of white men to display consideration and courtesy to the members of a coloured race. That intense Anglo-Saxon spirit of self-approbation which is unpleasantly perceptible in England itself, and is so often offensive among vulgar Englishmen on the Continent, very soon becomes rampant in India. Officials in India are far from being exempt from that weakness of human nature which is tickled by flattery and nourished by servile obsequiousness. Our Oriental subjects have pandered to this weakness, and, in accordance with the custom of Eastern countries, practise the profoundest adulation and abasement towards those set in authority over them. English officials, although they pretend to dislike this attitude, are secretly pleased at it, and do not hesitate to give open expression to their annoyance at its non-observance.

There are innumerable instances in which pedestrians have been abused and struck because they have not lowered their umbrellas at the sight of a sahib on the highway. There are few Indian gentlemen even of the highest rank who have not had experience of gross insults when travelling by railway, because Englishmen object to sit in the same carriage with a native. This form of insolence generally takes the shape of forcible ejection with all goods and chattels. In a *Times* review of the *Leaves from the Diaries of a Soldier and Sportsman*, by the late Sir Montagu Gerard, I read as follows :—"We have never read a book which shows more pertinently how the ruling caste, from sheer carelessness or from inbred contempt for the coloured races, lay themselves out to court unpopularity. Take two of his instances. A subaltern gets into a railway carriage, where, to his disgust, he finds a couple of Hindoo gentlemen. He quietly waits till the train is in motion, and then, as he expresses it, 'fires them out of the door.' A petty rajah, going on a state visit to Agra, takes his seat in a first-class compartment, with a magnificent send-off by his loyal subjects. On his return he sneaks out of the third-class, and explains to the expectant crowds that on the former occasion he had been boxed up with a couple of sahibs, muddy from snipe-shooting, who had made him shampoo them all the way." This story of the Indian rajah, who was called upon to unlace the boots and shampoo the weary legs of a British officer, is corroborated by Sir David Barr, the late Resident at Hyderabad, and would be incredible if it were not vouched for by such high authority. One does not know whether to marvel most at the insolence of the young subaltern or at the miserable spirit of the rajah, which induced him to submit to such abasement. But the incident illustrates the length to which British arrogance will go.

It is but too common an outrage to assault respectable residents of the country because when passing on the road they have not dismounted from their horses in token of their inferiority. I have known a case in which an unfortunate old man died from the effects of blows so received. The great shoe question, as it is called, has convulsed official society a hundred times. The comparative independence of the lads of the rising generation has excited in countless instances the ire of the officials who come in contact with them, and a crusade against the muslin-coated students of Bengal has culminated in many an unwise prosecution before a magistrate. It is with the extremest jealousy—notwithstanding their protestations in preference of a spirit of independence—that the official community has tolerated the omission by the natives of the country of any one of the extravagant signs of respect and humility to which it has hitherto been accustomed. But with the wide dissemination of English education and the growth of Western ideas it has been compelled to accept a change. "Men who speak better English than most Englishmen, who read Mill and Comte, Max Müller and Maine, who occupy with distinction seats on the judicial bench, who administer the affairs of native states with many millions of inhabitants, who manage cotton-mills and conduct the boldest operations of commerce, who edit newspapers in English and correspond on equal terms with the scholars of Europe—these can no longer be treated as an inferior breed."[1] They assert and exercise independence. They claim a position of equality with the ruling race. They demand to participate to an ever-increasing extent in the administration of their own affairs. They neglect to salaam to an Englishman when they meet him in the street, and they do not take off their shoes in his presence. Consciously or unconsciously, their attitude excites displeasure,

[1] It is a pleasure to me to quote this paragraph from my brother's monograph on *India*, in the English Citizen Series (Macmillan, 1883).

and is characterised by the rulers of the country as one of growing insolence.

It is a common thing to hear an English civilian now say: "No one can have a more kindly feeling towards the natives of the country than I have; I like the people; I like the masses; I like the up-country natives; but I cannot endure the Baboos." This puts the whole case in a nutshell. It is the Baboos who are the product of English education and civilisation. The public services as a body have no sympathy with the aspirations of the educated portion of the native community. The opposition to all proposals for the enlargement of India's liberties is headed by members of the Civil Service, and the unanimity of opposition is almost as marked among magistrates and judges as it is among planters, merchants, and members of other professions. The dislike to the educated natives of India is shared by all classes of Englishmen.

Yet those who know the Indians best will be the first to acknowledge the natural affection and gratefulness of their disposition. An Indian daily newspaper, published in Calcutta, contains some observations on this subject in a remarkable article entitled "Native attachment and gratitude to good, just, and noble-minded Englishmen," from which I make the following extract :—

It is a practical commentary on the truth and justice of the charge brought against natives, that they bitterly hate the dominant race as a rule, that individual attachment to individual Englishmen should be so marked a trait in native character. It is hardly possible to travel over any part of India where some individual Englishman has not left the impress of his hand, whether for good or evil, on the locality and its people. And it reflects the highest credit and honour on the native races that, while the names of the bad and oppressive men have almost been forgotten, the memory of the good, just, or charitable Englishman has been preserved by tradition in perfect freshness—a perpetual testimony to the simplicity, forgiving spirit, and gratitude of the Indian character. To hate bitterly is not in native nature. The native heart is naturally kind, but the kindness becomes warmer when the object of it is a member of the dominant class. It is not always because we expect any return from him, but it is a peculiar feeling with us to be anxious to stand well with a race to whom we owe so many obligations as a fallen and subject people. If those obligations had been unmixed with quite as great wrongs, it is our fear that Englishmen might have become objects of our idolatry, so enthusiastic is our regard and affection for all who really mean to confer or have conferred on us any great benefits.

It seems to me that there is little or no

exaggeration in these remarks; and for my own part I must say that I have often been astonished at the ebullitions of Indian gratitude which are so frequently evoked when English officials, who draw the whole of their salaries from India, have literally done no more than their bare duty by the people of the country in whose service they are employed. Any expression of real sympathy is always, in my experience, repaid by a hundredfold degree of respect and gratitude. As the *Indian Mirror* again observes in the same article:—

> It is utterly false to say, as has been said, that natives hate Englishmen as such. It is quite true that they do hate Europeans who miss no opportunity to scorn, abuse, and degrade them, or to injure them; but it is equally true that their respect and attachment to such men of Western races as do or mean to do them any good is almost unbounded.

If there is any increase of dislike between the two races, I must place on record my conviction that the people of India are not responsible for this aggravation of sentiment. It is due entirely to the changed circumstances in which the ruling race has found itself placed.

It would be strange, however, if there were not a reciprocity of dislike. The organs of Anglo-India have lately resented with some warmth the tendency of the English-speaking portion of the Indian community to speak and think of the British in India as "foreigners." The word strikes a jarring note and is naturally resented, but the tendency is undoubted. It is one symptom of the national awakening, of the rising spirit of patriotism, of the struggle for equality. The revolution which has been wrought by English influences and civilisation will always constitute the most abiding monument of British rule. The change is as complete as that which was effected by the Renaissance in Europe. It is hundred-armed, and leaves no side of the national character untouched. But the Government has been irresponsive: it remains the same, a monopoly of the ruling race, and so far from there being any real advance in the direction of popular concessions, a distinct reactionary impulse too often animates its counsels. There is no diminution of suspicion, distrust, and dislike of the national movement. The aim and end of the new Imperial policy is to knit with closer bonds the power of the British Empire over India, to proclaim and establish that supremacy through ceremonies of pomp and pageantry, and by means of British capital to exploit the country in the economic interests of the British nation.

The encouragement of Indian aspirations falls not within its ken. It would be strange indeed if the fire of a patriotic opposition were not kindled.

A sense of political disabilities is the dominant note of discontent among the educated classes, and to this has been superadded the consciousness of the economic evil which the exploitation of the country by foreign capital and foreign agencies inflicts on it. Their anti-official sentiment is due to their practical exclusion from participation in the higher official life of their country ; the anti-commercial feeling is due to their practical exclusion from participation in the higher walks of industrial and commercial life. The burning embers are slowly rising into a flame. There is a growing spirit of antagonism not less to the commercial than to the official representatives of British rule ; the great gulf which separates Englishmen from Indians is widening, and the increased bitterness of race feeling is now reflected by Indian as well as by English prejudice.

INDIAN LAND PROBLEMS

THERE is no country in the world where the land system presents a richer variety of forms than India, and there is no study which can have a deeper interest to the economist or present higher lessons to the statesman than a consideration of the administration of the land tax in that country.

English administrators have often blundered in India, because Englishmen are only familiar with their own system of landlord and tenant, of farmers and labourers who cultivate and are paid by wages. But the old and established land system of India is something very different from this. Whatever form of land tenure may prevail, the cultivator has enjoyed from time immemorial substantial customary rights in the soil he cultivates. The policy of our Indian administration has been, too often, to deny or ignore these rights. But there is in the village communities, the skeletons of which still survive, a privilege of property in the occupation or management of the soil which constitutes as strong a form of property as can anywhere be found ; and there still remains among the occupiers of land a distinct property therein, with specific rights entitling them to fixity of tenure and protection, and subject only to payment of the customary land tax. The occupancy ryots of Bengal, the peasant proprietors of Madras and Bombay, are born to the traditions of their respective land systems, and are as tenacious of their privileges as the freemen of our own country.

The land tax is levied by the State. The original form of this tax was a share of the produce in kind. When the crop was reaped, the State was entitled to a proportion of the grain, regulated according to the custom of the locality. That is a very old arrangement. In ancient times the proportion was a very small one—one-tenth or so ; but it has gradually been raised to the highest point at which it can be levied. It is needless to say that the tax is no longer paid in kind, but in cash. The proceeds constitute the land revenue, as it is called, and are in fact the most important financial asset in the Indian Budget. The assessment of this land tax is described in official language as a "settlement of land revenue." To the extent that the Indian Government imposes a heavy land tax, it may be said that the State in India is an illustration of State landlordism. But to that extent only, and no more. The State in India is not the superior proprietor in a sense with which we are familiar. The statement is sometimes made that the Government of India is a vast landed proprietor, and that the occupiers of the soil are its tenants. But there is no real truth in such a description, and the Government has no title to absolute ownership. All that it is entitled to is a certain share of the produce. That is the kernel of the situation, and all our difficulties in the land administration in India hang upon the misunderstanding or misrepresentation or misapplication of this essential condition.

In Bengal a distinctive land system has been preserved by the British Government. There is an educated and influential class of landlords —a body of middlemen between the State and the cultivator—who have identified themselves with British rule, and have always given loyal help in the cause of good administration. There is a strong and intelligent middle-class, holding tenures of various degrees under the landlords, and forming the strongest element in a progressive society. And there is a resourceful peasantry, able to defend their rights, and able also to resist the first effects of a drought and a failure of crops. The rents are light ; the cultivators are not under the thraldom of money-lenders ; and British administrators can view with a just pride a province where their moderation has assured agricultural prosperity to the people. The land tax is levied from the landlords ; it is fixed for ever, and the rights of the cultivators under the landlords are adequately protected by legislation. This system is known as the Permanent Settlement.

In Madras there is still some element of a landlord system, but in both Madras and Bombay it may be said, generally speaking, that the Government imposes its land tax direct upon the cultivators. It is a great misfortune that in these provinces the ancient and indigenous institution of village communities, which we found flourishing in full vigour at the beginning of our rule, should have been swept away. These communities were self-contained and self-governing little republics, and comprised in miniature all the materials of a State within themselves. It was a mistaken policy to efface these indigenous and self-governing bodies, and it was especially unwise to do so under an alien rule, which can never be in sympathetic touch with the people, except through their natural representatives. But they were everywhere ignored for the purpose of the land tax, in order to make settlements direct with cultivators. It was intended at first that the assessment upon these cultivators should be permanent, and that every cultivating proprietor should be permitted to hold his land at a fixed assessment for ever. If that principle had been maintained it would have afforded some relief. But it was not adhered to ; and it soon came to pass that the cultivators, who were at the mercy of the land assessors, were ground down to the dust. The Government stands over them, as John Bright said many years ago, "with a screw which is perpetually turned." They suffer from two of the greatest evils which can afflict agriculture, viz., over-assessment and uncertainty in the demand. The security which is given to the cultivator of Northern India is denied to the cultivator of Madras or Bombay ; the former can reckon beforehand on what definite ground his landlord can claim an increase of rent ; the latter does not know on what grounds the State will augment his land tax at the next settlement. Security and permanence are the essential conditions of productive energy, and indefiniteness and uncertainty paralyse agriculture. Uncertainty is, if possible, a greater evil than over-assessment, and human wit and ingenuity could devise no scheme better calculated to keep the peasantry of a country in a state of permanent penury and indebtedness than to subject them to enhancements on each recurring settlement, on grounds which are not defined, which cannot be contested, and which are not comprehended by the people.

This method of dealing with the cultivator direct is known as the *ryotwari* system, in contradistinction to the *zemindari* or landlord system of the Permanent Settlement. These are the two principal systems of land administration in India. There are many modifications of these systems ; in the Punjab, for instance, there is an excellent system of dealing with the cultivator through village communities ; and elsewhere arrangements are concluded on an elaborate basis for effecting temporary settlements with middlemen. But it is unnecessary for my purpose to discuss these variations. I pass on to general reflections which the principal systems of administration suggest.

There is no department of the Government to which more incessant and continuous attention is devoted than the administration and collection of the land tax. In no particular are we more ready to contrast British rule with Mogul rule so largely in our own favour as in our dealings with the land. We point to our equitable assessments as enhancing the value of landed property, to our agricultural experiments as increasing its productiveness, and to the benign protection of the British Government as enabling the ryot and his family to enjoy the fruits of their toil in unmolested quiet. But there is not one of these beliefs which is not delusive. Our dealings with the land have been more destructive of all ancient proprietary rights than were the old methods which preceded our own. Our rigid and revolutionary methods of exacting the land revenue have reduced the peasantry to the lowest extreme of poverty and wretchedness, and the procedure of our settlement courts has been the means of laying upon them burdens heavier than any they endured in former times. Famine is now more frequent than formerly and more severe, and it is the irony of fate that our statute-book is swollen with measures of relief in favour of the victims whom our administrative system has impoverished.

The primary cause of this state of things is the excessive departmental centralisation against which Sir James Caird many years ago vainly protested. No more complete type of a bureaucracy exists than the Indian Government, and, like all other bureaucracies, its members are driven to justify their own existence by extending the sphere of their activity. In old days our predecessors in the administration of the country, with more practical sagacity than we possess, were always cautious in their interference, and instinctively favoured the adoption of conservative principles. At the present time, when enormous advance has been made in the expansion of education, in the growth of political ideas, and in national development, the dead weight of administrative departments, needlessly multiplied, is prejudicial to real progress. Wise statesmanship would rather consist in the preservation of peace and order, and in the encouragement of spontaneous tendencies. What is needed is the decentralisation of the Government, the pervading presence of a spirit of relativity, of a capacity to refrain from unnecessary action, of an appreciation of the wide differences between the East and West, and between the different parts of India itself, and above all of a hearty sympathy with the wishes and interests of the governed. If these virtues are granted to the British rulers of India, we need not despair of seeing sound and healthy progress.

But unfortunately these virtues are rare, and in their place a spirit is abroad breathing disturbance. Ambitious officials, whose tenure of office is short, are consumed with a fatal desire to distinguish themselves by the enforcement of their own ideas, irrespective of the wishes and feelings of the people who are affected by them.

The experimental introduction of agrarian theories into a country altogether unripe for their application, where the existence of an aristocracy is still the material basis of order, and the maintenance of an hereditary land-holding class is the corner-stone of internal political reconstruction, is evidence of a profound unfitness to appreciate adequately the necessities of the existing situation. Far from leading through any healthy channels to the settlement of disputes, experiments of this sort are calculated to produce nothing but disorder, by setting up class against class in vain opposition to one another. The Indian tenancy laws, admirably framed as they are in many respects, are avowedly designed to subvert the old relations between zemindar and ryot, and to substitute a basis of contract for personal considerations. It is a common allegation that a large portion of the agrarian trouble existing in India is due to the old relations between landlord and tenant.

It is on this hypothesis that these laws have been enacted, and the Government of India has gone so far as to declare that "it would be failing in its duty to the future population of the country if, in order to secure the full development of its material resources twenty or fifty or even a hundred years sooner than it would otherwise come about, it deliberately introduced, while having power to exclude, the relation of landlord and tenant." I do not hesitate to affirm that this is a most dangerous doctrine, and that there is little foundation for this hypothesis of agrarian trouble. The social aspects of the land-tenure system of India are not those of Ireland or England or of any country in Western Europe. The system is not a perfect one, but it is the guarantee of social order among the agricultural classes. The normal relations of landlord and tenant rest upon a personal basis, and are independent of any conception of contract. It is true that rights are unadjusted, the balance of rent is undetermined, the current demand is not fixed, the area of cultivation is often unknown; and yet it is not the case that the ordinary relations between zemindar and ryot are unfriendly. The narrow induction drawn by local officials from occasional disturbances which come to their notice misleads them and has misled Government into the delusion that general disaffection exists. The one or two cases of disaffection come prominently to notice ; the thousands and thousands of instances in which order and contentment prevail pass by unobserved. The occasional agrarian disturbances to which so much importance has unduly been attached have for the most part been stirred up by the injudicious interference of zealous officials who are incapable of recognising the exigencies of the position in which they are placed. It cannot be too often repeated that a patrician aristocracy is the basis of internal order in India, to which the Government must always look for support and for the maintenance of its own duration and stability. The lower orders stand in urgent need of an aristocracy above them ; their ignorance and characteristic docility and want of firmness require the guidance and protection of more powerful superiors, and I am firmly convinced that the adoption of any policy to reduce the power of the dominant classes and to destroy distinctions in the different strata of society is fraught with danger to the State.

In this connection the opinion of the late Sir Henry Lawrence is worthy of attention, and a deep interest attaches to the following expression of his views, which is recorded in Sir Joseph

Fayrer's manuscript diary of the siege of Lucknow (quoted by Mr Forrest in his *Selections from Mutiny Despatches*, vol. ii. p. 63):—

> During the time that Sir Henry Lawrence was in my house before his death he talked frequently in an impressive but excited way, and amongst other things that he said, as his thoughts travelled from one subject to another, one which seemed to be most present to him was the causes of the Mutiny, and that which led to the troubles in which we were now involved. He spoke of the injudicious method in which native landholders had been dealt with by the Government, and, among other things, he said more than once with emphasis: "It was the John Lawrences, the Thomasons, the Edmonstones (and others) who brought India to this." This I heard distinctly.

Most important is it, for the safety of the State and the security of our rule, to conciliate the great body of landed proprietors, to attach to the British Government those persons whose influence is the most permanent and extensive, to render it their palpable interest to uphold duly constituted authority, and to give them a valuable and abiding stake in the administration of the country.

The prosperity of every country requires that there should exist within it not only a proletariat, the great body of the people who devote themselves to labour, but also a class of capitalists who provide the funds which enable labour to become reproductive. It is the combination of capital and labour which leads to wealth: capital without labour is sterilised, and it is only under the fertilising influence of capital that labour is productive. It is not to the advantage of any country that it should consist exclusively of petty agriculturists whose rent is increased with increased production, and who will labour, therefore, neither for the improvement of the land nor for the extension of cultivation. It is not to the advantage of any people that they should be reduced to one dead level of a peasant proletariat, with no substantial middle-class such as forms the backbone of the nation in more favoured countries, and no upper-class on whom they can lean for assistance during an emergency. The Government of India, when it rejects the intervention of middlemen, acts as a rent-receiver only ; it is unable to sympathise with individual cases of misfortune among its tenants ; it is not disposed to invest any portion of its revenues in agricultural improvement ; it does not acknowledge and it certainly does not fulfil the duties of a capitalist landlord. It does not allow the profits of the soil to be distributed through the various grades of the community between the cultivator and the State. They pass into the coffers of the Government direct, and the people are only permitted to share among themselves the subsistence margin that is left.

One of the principal merits of the old native rule in India was the elasticity of its revenue system. The demand of rent or revenue was not rigid or fixed, but variable with the seasons and the distress or prosperity of the people. In a favourable year large collections would be made; when the crops had failed the demand would be reduced accordingly. We see the same principle now governing the land-revenue administration of the feudatory States, and it is a common reflection, echoed by all Indian gentlemen who have had experience in the management of those States, that it tends to the establishment of sympathy and friendliness. The same principle still controls the relation between landlord and tenant in British India. It is only in the most prosperous years that a full demand of rent is ever collected from the tenantry, and it may be taken as an ascertained fact that 75 per cent. on the demand is a fair average proportion of realisation in zemindari estates. This is a striking contrast to the practice in Government estates, where a full cent. per cent. on the current demand is rigidly exacted.

Nor does the Government system tend to develop the wealth of the peasantry by extension of cultivation. It was estimated by Lord Cornwallis that at the time of the permanent settlement of Bengal one-third of the culturable area of the province was waste and jungle. And yet within two generations, under the beneficent operation of that settlement, these waste lands were cultivated in every direction, and teeming agricultural wealth is now produced every year in tracts of country which formerly were wilderness or devastated by famine. These reclaimers of the jungle are all sub-tenure holders who have got land to clear on favourable terms from the zemindars or landlords of the parent estate, and have acquired an indefeasible title to the land they occupy. With the aid of a fertile soil, rising prices, and a continually increasing demand for produce, this system has proved extraordinarily successful.

Very different influences have been at work in provinces where the land is held directly by the State. The soil is not less fertile, and the cultivators have the same stimulus in respect of rising prices and the increasing demand for produce, but they are labouring under the burden of a system in which the land is periodically settled with them by Government. This system has not promoted the cultivation of the country, and the prohibition of sub-letting has proved fatal to the extension of land reclamation. So true is it that a proprietary tenure, if left in the hands of the people, will always be fruitful, but that if retained by Government it starves.

In a country like India, where almost the entire community is agricultural, all questions relating to land are of the most engrossing interest to the people, and the attitude of Government for good or evil is the source of prosperity or the cause of suffering. Nothing is more needful than that we should forbear from casting about for every opportunity of exacting from the cultivators more and more of the fruits of their labour, and that we should desist from fanciful innovations, which always imply harassment and disturbance. Nothing is more urgently necessary than that there should be a reasonable, equitable, and intelligible limit to the State demand, and that greater elasticity, in accordance with the old Indian custom, should be allowed in the operations of the taxgatherers.

Under the viceroyalty of Lord Canning a bold attempt was made to effect improvement. But the pendulum of official opinion soon swung back, and the subsequent efforts of Lord Ripon in this direction were frustrated. More recently Lord Curzon has followed with some concessions for which we may be grateful, but they were bought too late at the cost of much suffering, and the newly-found toleration, which was forced on the Government by outside agitation, cannot be recognised as adequate. No protection has been afforded against excessive assessment or undue enhancement. No attempt is made to adjust the revenue or rent demand so that it may represent any fixed proportion of the produce of the land or of its letting value; and the amount of the assessment to be imposed on an individual unit is determined chiefly by a consideration of the percentage of increase which can safely be exacted from the area under settlement. The limits placed by law on enhancements claimed by private landlords have not been extended to cases where the State is the landlord, and peasant proprietors paying revenue to the State have not been allowed the civil remedy which tenants of private landlords enjoy. "The true function of Government is to lay down broad and generous principles for the guidance of its officers, with becoming regard to the traditions of the province and the circumstances of the locality, and to prescribe moderation in enhancement and sympathy in collection." These are the admirable sentiments enunciated by Lord Curzon for the amelioration of the Indian system of land revenue policy. They should be engraved on tablets of brass over the council-chambers of India, as the speech of the Emperor Claudius was engraved at Lugdunum. But alas that practice should so lag behind the precept! It is a mockery to preach of "moderation in enhancement and sympathy in collection" when re-settlements and survey, with their symbols of oppression, the theodolite and compass, the initiation of incessant local inquiries for the assessment of land, however small, and the realisation of Government demands by summary process, are resorted to with no less frequence than formerly, and with no diminution of harshness or persistence.

Not less injudicious is the policy of interference with old customs and economic conditions. Those conditions vary from one another as widely as the *petite culture* of France differs from the system of large proprietary holdings and farms in England. And yet we insist on introducing one nomenclature, to which, like the bed of Procrustes, we adapt all tenures, holdings, and systems of settling the Government demand of revenue and rent. These administrative fictions, which proceed on the assumption that what is true of one part of a province must be applicable to the whole, are a prolific source of trouble. A blind adhesion to theoretic symmetry will always lead to practical confusion. And so it has come to pass that the principal officers of the revenue department have been mobbed by despairing ryots in the streets of Calcutta, and compelled to revise settlements, reduce assessments, and remit revenue demands which ought never to have been made. I may be allowed to refer to a case of which I possess particular knowledge. For more than a century an invariable custom had been followed in the assessment of waste lands brought under cultivation in the Chittagong district, and during this long period the Government had concluded more than 50,000 settlements with individual tenure-holders on one consistent principle. But when that principle was completely reversed, and I protested against the change, I was called upon to show that Government was in any way pledged to follow the old procedure in future settlements. I replied then, as I reply now, that I was not concerned to meet the challenge. I claim that there should be some continuity in administration, and that present and future Governments should show some respect for precedent, customs, and rights invariably recognised by their predecessors. I deprecate the shifts and changes to which it is so often proposed to subject our revenue policy, as inevitably exercising a most injurious effect upon the people who are the victims of our experiment. Is it to be supposed that such changes will play innocuously, so to speak, over the heads of the agricultural classes? This is assuredly the only aspect with which true statesmanship would concern itself; but by our revenue authorities it is too often wholly ignored, or buried in a multitude of circular instructions which lead only to the increasing harassment of an already overburdened peasantry.

Even more serious cause for anxiety is the suppressed premise, which runs through all our revenue policy, that the soil of the country does not belong to the inhabitants of the country, but to the Government. There may be no great harm in saying that the land belongs to "the State" when the State is only another name for the people, but it is very different when the State is represented by a small minority of foreigners, who disburse nearly one-third of the revenues received from the land on the remuneration of their own servants, and who have no abiding-place on the soil and no stake in the fortunes of the country. By vigorously assuming the false position that a party of foreign occupiers who choose to call themselves "the State" have become the proprietors of the actual soil of India, we have depreciated all other rights of property therein ; we have subverted the entire organisation of the village communities ; we have torn up by the roots the economic fabric by which the agricultural classes of the country were held together ; and we have substituted in its place a costly and mechanical centralisation. Our Mogul predecessors were content to levy the State demand by simple processes which had grown up imperceptibly with the administration, and were sanctioned by immemorial usage. The harshness and cruelty of the Mogul taxgatherers, on which we are too prone to dwell, were tempered by the contingency of migration, which effectually acted as a check upon oppressive landlords. The rapacity of Oriental despotism was restrained by the self-interest of those who were employed on the assessment and collection of the taxes. The old records of our English Government are full of evidence that the fixed and unbending system which we introduced in place of existing arrangements was profoundly disliked by the people.[1] We aimed at an impossible perfection and mastery of detail ; we have succeeded only in creating disturbance. Short settlements, an exacting demand, and an unbending severity in collecting rent have driven the simple husbandmen into the clutches of the money-lender, and are responsible for their share in intensifying the effects of famine. It is only in Bengal, which for the most part has received the boon of a permanent settlement, and where a large and influential body of landlords intervenes between the Government and the people, that the peasantry are not impoverished, and that measures of relief are rarely, if ever, necessary.

There remains the question of the improvement of agriculture. Whatever wealth there is in India is obtained from the soil, and the importance, therefore, of making two blades of corn grow where one grew before is almost incalcu-

[1] Take by way of illustration the following extract from Dr Buchanan's *Statistical Survey*, Book IV. chap. vii., on the district of Dinajepore, which is quoted in the Fifth Report (1812):—"The natives allege that although they were often squeezed by the Mogul officers, and on all occasions were treated with the utmost contempt, they preferred suffering these evils to the mode that has been adopted of selling their lands when they fall into arrears, which is a practice they cannot endure. Besides, bribery went a great way on most occasions, and they allege that, bribes included, they did not actually pay one-half of what they do now."

lable. It is mere justice to say that the Government of India has never been blind to this importance. We hear now, as we have often heard before, that a body of experts and chemists has been associated with the various agricultural departments, that an agricultural research laboratory has been organised, and that, in connection with the laboratory, an agricultural college and a large experimental farm has been established, "so that the theory and science and practice of agriculture can be progressively taught." There is nothing new in these schemes; they have been put forward a score of times, and experimental or model farms have again and again been multiplied in all parts of India. I can remember no period when this question has not engaged the attention of Government, and when active steps have not been taken for the development of agricultural inquiries and experiments. But all these attempts have been destined to fail. Elaborate and costly departments have been created, but the indigenous methods of agriculture have not been improved one jot or tittle by official enterprise. The ryots of India possess an amount of knowledge and practical skill within their own humble sphere which no expert scientist can ever hope to acquire. Our attempts to teach the natives of India agriculture are based upon a forgetfulness of the essential elements of the case. The native cultivators of India are too poor to be able to adopt the scientific improvements which English experience suggests. They are told to plough deeper, to do more than scratch the soil. But it is forgotten that the cattle with which they plough are incapable of deep ploughing. We tell them to enrich their fields with manure, and that the produce of the land would be augmented by its use. No doubt it would. The ryots do utilise manure as much as they possibly can, in the way of simple forms of manure, such as cow-dung—which is, however, also an extremely useful article to the poor cultivator as a substitute for firewood—but they can no more afford to procure the expensive manures with which we are so familiar than they can afford to plough with elephants.

It is not in the power of the Government to effect any improvement by experiments in agriculture, or by agricultural teaching, or by any form of departmental interference. I do not know whether the poverty of the people does not always obtrude as a permanent obstacle to improvement. But of this I feel sure, that all attempt to lead should be given up, and that our object should be little more than the arrangement of agricultural facts from which the awakened intelligence of the Indian community may in due course profit to its own advantage. If the agricultural departments succeed in laying a foundation of scientific knowledge and in enlisting the sympathy of Indian gentlemen in the welfare of the agricultural classes by assisting them to better knowledge, they will not have been constituted in vain. The ambition of those departments should be to secure the active aid of members of the Indian community who are sincerely interested in agriculture.[1] It is only through and by the Indian community that agricultural improvements can on any important scale be effected. There are landholders who have experience and facilities for extending improvements which no official can ever obtain, and many of them have capital available for investment in agricultural enterprise. They are familiar with the usages of the agricultural classes. They understand the existing systems of Indian agriculture, and are acquainted with the local reasons which justify practices that may seem strange and illogical to an English observer. They can therefore best guide the course of

[1] These principles were enunciated in one of Lord Ripon's resolutions, dated 8th December 1881, but they have not been acted up to.

agricultural improvement with the least disturbance of existing circumstances, and develop the true policy of progress in improving and adding to indigenous conditions without that subversion of ideas and methods which inevitably accompanies the introduction of exotic experiments.

INDIA'S ECONOMIC PROBLEM

THE greatest material boon which could be conferred on India would be the restoration of her industries. The greatest material calamity which can befall India is that which has been going on for so many years before our eyes—the continual contraction of her manufactures. The agricultural trade of India has expanded, but her manufactures have diminished: the imports of cotton piece-goods, which forty years ago were valued at 8½ millions sterling, now exceed 23 millions; the ancient weaving industry has been practically extinguished and the local manufactures of the country have been crushed out by British competition. The tendency of events for more than a century has been to turn the people more and more towards agriculture, and less and less to manufactures. While the invention of steam engines and the development of machinery enormously cheapened the cost of production in England, the operation of transit duties in India, amounting to £450,000 per annum, and of heavy and ruinous import duties in England, amounting to 67 per cent. and more, on the value of cotton and silk goods, combined to repress all the exertions of local industry. These duties, which were deliberately imposed in order to enable English manufacturers to undersell the Indian artisan, have long ago been repealed, but they did their work. The introduction of Manchester goods has been accompanied by the collapse of indigenous industries.

Mr Henry St George Tucker, a Director of the Honourable East India Company, wrote as long ago as 1823:—

> What is the commerce which we have adopted in this country with relation to India? The silk manufactures and its piece-goods made of silk and cotton intermixed have long since been excluded altogether from our markets; and of late, partly in consequence of the operation of a duty of 67 per cent., but chiefly from the effect of superior machinery, the cotton fabrics, which hitherto continued the staple of India, have not only been displaced in this country, but we actually export our cotton manufactures to supply a part of the consumption of our Asian possessions. India is thus reduced from the state of a manufacturing country to that of an agricultural country.

Even more emphatic is the verdict of Professor Horace Hayman Wilson, the historian of India:—

It was stated in evidence (1813) that the cotton and silk goods of India up to that period could be sold for a profit in the British market at a price from 50 to 60 per cent. lower than those fabricated in England. It consequently became necessary to protect the latter by duties of 70 and 80 per cent. on their value, or by positive prohibition. Had this not been the case, had not such prohibitory duties and decrees existed, the mills of Paisley and Manchester would have been stopped in their outset, and could scarcely have been again set in motion, even by the power of steam. They were created by the sacrifice of Indian manufactures. Had India been independent, she would have retaliated, would have imposed prohibitive duties upon British goods, and would thus have preserved her own productive industry from annihilation. This act of self-defence was not permitted her; she was at the mercy of the stranger. British goods were forced upon her without paying any duty, and the foreign manufacturer employed the arm of political injustice to keep down and ultimately strangle a competitor with whom he could not have contended on equal terms.

And yet the manufactures of India were once in a highly flourishing condition. The Mogul Courts enouraged large towns and urban enterprise. European traders were first attracted to India, not by its raw products, but by its manufactured wares. It was the industrial "wealth of Ormuz and Ind" that dazzled the eyes of Western nations and sent them in search of a passage to that land of fabulous prosperity. Large portions of the Indian population were engaged in various industries down to the close of the eighteenth century. In the palmy days of the Honourable East India Company a certain part of the revenues of the country was set aside to be employed in the purchase of goods for exportation to England, which was called the investment. But the commercial agents of the Company were not engaged in exploiting the resources of the soil, and the "upcountry investment" was entirely devoted to the purchase of manufactures. Nor was India at that time dependent on its maritime commerce. The inland trade was very considerable. The fame of the fine muslins of Bengal, her rich silks and brocades, her harmonious cotton prints, had spread far and wide in Asia as well as Europe. "The Bengal silks, cloths, etc.," writes Mr Verelst, who was Governor of Bengal before Hastings, "were dispersed to a vast amount to the west and north, inland as far as Guzerat, Lahore, and even Ispahan." The Indian cities were populous and magnificent.

When Clive entered Murshedabad, the old capital of Bengal, he wrote of it: "This city is as extensive, populous, and rich as the city of London, with this difference, that there are individuals in the first possessing infinitely greater property than in the last city." All the arts then flourished, and with them urban life. Now, out of a population of three hundred millions, only 7 per cent. live in towns of more than 10,000 inhabitants. In Ireland, that unfortunate annexe of the British dominions, the proportion is about 20, in Scotland it is 50, and in England and Wales it is 67 per cent. An overwhelming majority of the people of India live in rural villages, and the colonies of workmen who were settled in the large towns have been broken up.

I will cite as an example the city of Dacca. It was during the time of the Mogul government that this city reached the zenith of its prosperity. When it passed under British administration the population was estimated at two hundred thousand souls. In 1787 the exports of Dacca muslin to England amounted to £300,000; in 1817 they had ceased altogether. The arts of spinning and weaving, which for ages afforded employment to a numerous and industrious population, have now become extinct. Families which were formerly in a state of affluence have been reduced to penury: the majority of the people have been driven to desert the town and betake themselves to the villages for a livelihood. The present population of the town of Dacca is slowly increasing, but it is only 90,500.

This decadence has occurred in all parts of India, and not a year passes in which the local officers do not bring to the notice of Government that the manufacturing classes are becoming impoverished. The most profitable Indian industries have been destroyed and the most valuable Indian arts have greatly deteriorated. Dyeing, carpet-making, fine embroidery, jewellery, metal-work, the damascening of arms, carving, paper-making, even architecture and sculpture have decayed. "There is no class," exclaims Sir James Caird, "which our rule has pressed harder upon than the native weaver and artisan." I doubt whether the public at large has any conception of the deplorably small proportion of persons in India who are dependent on art or commerce or mechanical production, or working or dealing in mineral products. The figures cannot be ascertained with precise accuracy, but I work out the proportion at about 15 per cent. in India, against about 80 per cent.

in the United Kingdom. The economic problem of India is the poverty of her people. The development of petty occupations and menial employment, the establishment of large industries capitalised by Englishmen, even the accumulation of silver, which has so depreciated in value, the increased use of brass pots, cheap cotton cloths, and umbrellas among the people, afford but a poor compensation for the variety of social and industrial life once spread through the country. The dimensions of Indian trade are not inconsiderable, and yet no country is more poor. The economic conditions upon which material prosperity depends are lacking. An India supplying England with its raw products, and in its turn dependent upon England for all its more important manufactures, is not a spectacle which is likely to reconcile an Indian patriot to the loss of the subtle and refined Oriental arts, the very secret of which has passed away; to the disappearance of innumerable weavers who have perished from starvation or have sunk for ever to the lot of agricultural labourers; or to the sacrifice of that constructive genius and mechanical ability which designed the canal system of Upper India and the Taj at Agra.

It is true that railways, cotton mills and jute mills, gold mining and coal mining, oil wells and refineries, have lately come into existence. But, with the exception of most of the cotton mills and a few of the coal mines, the operations are in alien hands ; the capital is British, and the profits do not remain in India. It is true also that in some minor trades and industrial professions there has been an increase in recent years. There are more shoemakers now, more carpenters, more tailors, more blacksmiths. The demand for shoes, furniture, clothes, ironware, and the like has increased. New wants have arisen, and facilities have been afforded for their gratification. The immense cheapening of cotton piece-goods and of other articles imported from Europe cannot be without its benefit to the country. But all this is not inconsistent with the growing poverty of the people, to which the unanimous testimony of Indian observers bears witness. This has been the theme of every National and Provincial Congress. It is supported by the evidence of Indian merchants and traders, who are convinced from their business experience that the struggle for existence is greater than it was before. Official opinion admits this in regard to artisans, but denies it in respect of the great mass of the population, the agricultural classes. The official verdict affirms that the material prosperity of the people generally has improved. This verdict is directly opposed to educated Indian opinion, and a battle royal rages between the contending camps. In any case, there is no question that the people of India are miserably poor. They are absolutely and relatively poor. A general survey of the Empire led Sir Robert Giffen, in his address to the British Association in 1903, to consider "how vast must be the economic gulf separating the people of the United Kingdom and the self-governing Colonies from India and like parts of the Empire occupied by subject races, when we find that forty-two millions of people in the United Kingdom consume in food and drink alone an amount equal to the whole income of three hundred millions of people in India." It is enough to repeat Lord Curzon's estimate that the aggregate income per head of the population is about £2 per annum.

For my part, I may be allowed to say that I believe in no general improvement. There has undoubtedly been improvement in some places: in Eastern Bengal, for instance, where the people are favoured with a fertile soil and a permanent settlement, where the demand for jute is practically unlimited and the rainfall never fails; in Burmah, where, with so much waste land, there has been a vast extension of rice cultivation;

and in tracts, such as those in the Punjab and elsewhere, which have been fertilised by irrigation. But I can find no sign of general improvement. The increasing number of families and the terrible mortality which results from them, in spite of all the exertions of the Government and the heroic effort of individual officers, are—if there were no other evidence—an overwhelming demonstration that the capacity of the people to maintain themselves is on the decline. It is no argument to reply that there was heavy mortality from famine in ancient times. There was : the rains failed them as they fail now, the crops withered, and the people perished because there was no food to support them. There was then no means of conveying food to the afflicted province. But now, with improved communications, there is never any deficiency in the supply of food. The failure of the rains no longer means famine, for grain can be and always is imported into the distressed tracts. Famine ensues because the people are too poor to buy food. We no longer hear the old story of crowds perishing with money in their hands. At the same time, owing to improved communications, the reserves of food-grain have everywhere been depleted. The old custom was for the peasantry to keep among themselves three-quarters of a year's supply. Now the surplus is always exported, and there are no stores to fall back upon in the hour of need. The deficiency is imported at a price the people cannot afford to pay. The reason why famines are more frequent now than formerly, and more severe, is that the resources of the people are less able to resist them.

The increasing poverty of India is due to many causes, but primarily I trace it to the decay of handicrafts and the substitution of foreign for home manufactures. It is due also to the extension of agriculture. Every exertion is made to augment the area under cultivation with staple crops, and the increase in the amount of agricultural produce exported is pointed to as irrefragable proof of increased national prosperity. It is a proof of the reverse. Foreign markets are forced and commodities are sold at a lower rate—take tea, for example—and bought at a higher price than would otherwise be necessary. The export trade has indeed been developed at a great cost, and in the meanwhile the soil of the country has been impoverished by overcropping, and the breed of cattle is deteriorating from want of pasturage. The blessing has been withheld from the parched fields. Nor, unfortunately, does the profit from increased exports find its way, as it should, to the pockets of the cultivators. On the contrary, they receive but little of it themselves, for their crops are ordinarily mortgaged before being harvested, and the profit goes to middlemen. In all times, no doubt, the bulk of the Indian population has been agricultural, but formerly the cultivators were not wholly dependent on agriculture. They had home industries which employed their leisure when labour in the fields was useless; there was the carrying trade, in which the bullocks used at other times for ploughing were employed—the railroads have very much ruined this trade; and, above all, there was the weaving industry. The ryots are now reduced to the simple labour of their fields. "No one," said Lord Ripon at the opening of the Exhibition of Industrial Arts in Calcutta in 1884, "No one who considers the economic condition of India can doubt that one of its greatest evils is to be found in the fact that the great mass of the people of the country are dependent almost exclusively upon the cultivation of the soil. The circumstance tends at one and the same time to depress the position of the cultivators, to aggravate the evils of famine, and also to lower wages generally." I will add that it tends also to maintain them in the depths of ignorance in which they are sunk. It will always be found in all countries that the artisans are more highly educated than the peasantry.

A further cause of the impoverishment of India is the drain from the country. Before the Mutiny, the sums annually drawn from India by Great Britain amounted to two or three millions only. The Home Charges alone now exceed eighteen millions, of which nine millions and three quarters are on account of interest on funded and railway debt, and four millions four hundred and sixty thousand pounds are on account of pensions paid in England. These charges increase year by year. But this grand total does not include the remittances on account of private gains from railways, banking, merchandise, the ocean and river carrying trade, tea and coffee planting, cotton and jute mills, indigo, coal mines, and the like, or the private savings of officials and others which are sent to England. Taking these into consideration, it is a moderate computation that the annual drafts from India to Great Britain amount to a total of thirty millions. The equivalent of this at the current rate of exchange is four hundred and fifty million rupees. It can never be to the advantage of the people of India to remit annually this enormous sum to a foreign country. The amount paid in pensions may be inevitable, but it is obviously a dead loss, for it is spent abroad; and no country was ever a prosperous one in which the interest payable on its own capital expenditure, whether for military purposes or on reproductive public works, was not distributed among its own people. Only 10 per cent. of the public debt of India is held in India itself. There is a constant drain from India to pay the interest on the remaining 90 per cent., which is held in the United Kingdom. There is a constant drain also to pay the profits which are remitted to England on account of the investment of British capital in India.

Lord Curzon very forcibly said, in a speech delivered by him in November 1902, at Jaipore: "There is no spectacle which finds less favour in my eyes or which I have done more to discourage than that of a cluster of Europeans settling down upon a Native State and sucking from it the moisture which ought to give sustenance to its own people." *Rem acu tetigisti*, I exclaim; but I add, in the words of the same old satirist, *Mutato nomine de te fabula narratur*. Lord Curzon lost sight of the fact that what is true of the Native States is true also of the whole of India. In a speech to the Bengal Chamber of Commerce at Calcutta in the ensuing February, he sneered at India's economic drain as a "copy-book fallacy" and as "a foolish and dangerous illusion." But how can it be denied that it would be vastly more beneficial to India if the wealth produced in the country were spent in the country? India is the field where capital is invested, but all the interest that is reaped therefrom passes to the pocket of the investor, and he takes it to England. To say that it makes no difference to India whether the wealth made in India is taken away elsewhere or spent in the country itself is not the doctrine of economic science, nor is it the language of common-sense. India is not inhabited by a savage primitive people who have reared no indigenous system of industry or art, who are ignorant of their own interests, and who are incapable of advance in civilisation.[1] They look back on their past with

[1] I cannot refrain from reproducing the noble panegyric of Burke in the speech on the East India Bill:—

"This multitude of men does not consist of an abject and barbarous populace, much less of gangs of savages like the Guaranies and Chiquitos who wander on the waste borders of the river of Amazon or the Plate; but a people for ages civilised and cultivated by all the arts of polished life whilst we were yet in the woods. There have been (and still the skeletons remain) princes once of great dignity, authority, and opulence. There are to be found the chiefs of tribes and nations. There is to be found an ancient, venerable priesthood, the depository of their laws, learning, and history, the guides of the people whilst living and their consolation in death; a nobility of great antiquity and renown; a multitude of cities not exceeded in population and trade by those of the first class in

a just sense of pride, and under the influence of English education are stimulated with new aspirations and legitimate ambition. India is poor, and there are those who believe that in consequence of its political conditions it is becoming poorer; but the ambition of its people is to take their place among other nations in the future federation of the world. They are convinced that the prosperity of their country depends on the diminution of its economic drain and on the conservation of its resources for ultimate development by indigenous agency. Their opposition to the exploitation of their country by foreigners is based upon their conviction that this exploitation is a real obstacle to their progress and a source of present and future trouble to their nation.

Another source of impoverishment is the artificial exchange which has been established in the Indian currency. While the silver value of the rupee remains at about tenpence, its artificial value has been fixed at a convertibility of one shilling and fourpence into gold. At

Europe; merchants and bankers who have once vied in capital with the Bank of England, whose credit has often supported a tottering State and preserved their governments in the midst of war and desolation; millions of indigenous manufacturers and mechanics; millions of the most diligent and not of the least intelligent tillers of the earth."

the same time the purchasing power of the rupee, according to all the tests which can be applied in regard to its power of purchasing food-grains, has not increased, but on the contrary has declined. The total value of the annual exports of Indian merchandise exceeds a thousand millions of rupees. But if the intrinsic or silver value of the rupee be taken, the value must be raised by 40 per cent., and to this extent the producers and factors are deprived of the legitimate price of their produce. No doubt in that case the purchasing power of the rupee would further fall, and every item of expenditure be ultimately forced up, but the process of depreciation is a slow one, and for a generation at least the producer in India would have been a gainer. The Government has profited immensely by the artificial raising of the rupee, as it is able to pay its interest on sterling loans at a lower rate of remittance ; the officials as a body and other persons who draw their salaries in silver have also profited ; but on the other hand the bulk of the people and all classes of producers are injuriously affected by this cause —the European tea-planter as well as the grower of jute, oil-seeds, and food-grains. The masses of the community in India have also suffered in many other ways by the closure of the mints. The value of the rupee having been raised, the agriculturists pay a higher rent and the people generally contribute to the taxes of the country in an appreciated currency. It was this point the Hon. Mr Gokhale drove home in the memorable speech delivered by him in March 1902 in the Viceroy's Council, at Calcutta, when he argued that the surpluses of the Indian revenues were due to the artificial currency policy of the Government, and that the present rate of taxation ought, therefore, to be reduced. There was no one who could answer him on that issue.

What, then, is the remedy? It is easier to diagnose the disease than to cure it. I do not pretend to offer a panacea cut and dried for the solution of the difficulties of the economic revolution through which India is passing. But of one thing we may be assured: that they can never be overcome except by the systematic encouragement of indigenous arts and industries, and by the introduction of mechanical appliances. These, again, can never be fully utilised until the children of the soil have been prepared for their use by technical education. The value of agitation in this direction is therefore evident. But I must add the essential caution that it is only one side of the question with which technical education deals: that is only one of the agencies by which India will be assisted in recovering her economic equilibrium; it must not be pressed prematurely. The clerical or literary professions are said to be overstocked. But there is still a large demand holding out prospects of the most attractive employment in such professions as law, medicine, or Government service. The service of Government in particular possesses potent charms which I at least have no cause to undervalue, and I have no sympathy with the practice so much in vogue of denouncing the natural aspiration of Indian students to obtain an appointment in the service of their own country. It is urged upon these students to drop their exclusive devotion to so-called liberal education and to devote themselves to a course of technical instruction. But it is the simple truth when I say that there is at present no prospect of employment or emolument for them, be they never so profoundly trained in the highest branches of science, or in the most elaborate technical accomplishments. We must look at these matters as practical men would look at them. The great drawback to technical education, as it is now being urged in India, is that it affords no sufficiently remunerative opening and no satisfactory outlet for an independent career. In the absence of capital, the only support which will give life to the current movement is the guarantee of Government employment. There is, of course, no such guarantee. I would not be understood to discourage the endowment of colleges of science, schools of art, and technological institutes. Far from it. The accumulation of capital would be paralysed if there were not this technical training to facilitate its use. But let us be careful that our zeal for these institutions does not lead us into the untenable position of stimulating a supply for which there is at present no natural demand.

What is more necessary is to stimulate the demand, and how this can best be done is the problem for solution. The demand for technical education can only be expanded by the application of capital. But where is the capital to come from? India is a poor country, and the only rich men to be found are, as a rule, wealthy landlords, who are constitutionally indisposed to invest their money in industrial enterprise. From every point of view we are confronted with the staggering poverty of our Indian fellow-subjects. Mr Reginald Murray, a well-known Calcutta banker, has been at the pains of getting together some figures showing the relative extent to which banking is carried on in England and in India. With a population of forty-two millions, there are in the 6025 offices of the United Kingdom deposits equal to a contribution per head of twenty pounds. India, with a population of three hundred millions, has only 127 banks, and the deposits per head of the population are twenty-four pence. For this the people themselves are to some extent to blame. There is no doubt that the progress of the country is greatly hampered by the national custom of hoarding. The quantity of this hoarded wealth has been enormously exaggerated, and but little of it is available for useful purposes. A sense of distrust induces petty traders to shrink from depositing their money with bankers, and their resources are too scattered and distributed in too small quantities to be of much utility for profitable investment. Still, there is substantial foundation for the charge of wasted capital. Both silver and gold are hoarded in specie and converted into ornaments to an extent altogether opposed to the best interests of the people; and so long as individuals who understand the use of capital, as well as those who do not, permit themselves and encourage others to sink their savings and even to borrow money for deposit in this unproductive manner, it is a truism to declare that wealth decreases and prosperity decays. An urgent need in India, therefore, is the better disposition of hoarded wealth, of men who will not fritter away their money on marriage expenses or ceremonies, and are not unwilling to lay out capital on undertakings which will bring them neither titles nor official smiles. We do not want capital to be buried or squandered.

It is not only the perverse use of capital with which we have to contend: it is always the poverty of the country that is arrayed against us as our most formidable opponent. It is to labour-saving appliances, to the action of machinery, that we must look for any considerable advancement in technical skill. The standard of living among the labouring classes of India is, however, so low, that unless machinery is introduced in a somewhat wholesale manner, their very poverty will place them in a position to withstand its competition. The cost of production by manual labour is so cheap that the introduction of machines is rendered difficult. Above all, the workmen of India are themselves in the habit of raising their own small capital, and have never been accustomed to work under large capitalists for bare wages after the manner of European artisans. They are still labouring under the conditions of a primitive industrial system which has disappeared from Western countries. The introduction of machinery will require a readjustment of the relations of capital and labour on a larger scale than accompanied the revolution inaugurated by the discoveries of Watt and Arkwright. The problem is by no means easy. The most permanent remedy appears to be in industrial co-operation and organisation for the purpose of raising joint capital. This is a practical proposal, but it raises, I fear, a somewhat distant prospect of realisation. I welcome the suggestions put forward for the establishment of village banks on the basis of co-operative credit, and am glad that some beginning in this direction has already been made; I rejoice that legislation for giving a legal status to village banks has at last been undertaken. Or we may turn to the establishment of a National Bank, and of subsidiary local banks on the lines which have been adopted with such success by Lord Cromer in Egypt. The relations of these banks with the State are few; their rate of interest is low, and the aid of the Government is invoked only for the realisation of outstanding dues. If the Government of India were to follow the example which has been set to them in Egypt, there might be some hope of raising capital and ameliorating the conditions of Indian industrial finance.

Lastly, there is not only the poverty but the ignorance of the Indian workman which we have to face. There is an obvious need for securing greater intelligence in the direction of industry than can be expected of illiterate labourers. The total expenditure on primary education in India from the funds of the State at the present time does not exceed two hundred thousand pounds. There is no free education, still less is it compulsory. Not more than one-sixth of the number of boys of school-going age are attending school, and there is only one primary school to five villages. This matter lies at the root of the poverty of the country, the remedy rests entirely in the hands of the Government of the country ; and of all the immediate difficulties in the way of alleviating the misery of the people, it is the easiest to surmount.

A proposal which is advocated with persistent vigour by the Indian press is that the Government should afford assistance to indigenous industries by protection. We have lately seen the introduction of protective legislation in the interest of the tea industry, and both the tea and the indigo industries are being bolstered up by the State with money grants for the encouragement of scientific observation and teaching. So much for industries under the management of Europeans, and it is not surprising that a cry should arise for the protection and encouragement of enterprises in which Indians take the lead. Why should Government undertake for the benefit of the planters to tax exported tea, with a view to placing funds at the disposal of the industry in order to push the sale of Indian tea, and refuse to impose a similar tax for the benefit of any other industry which may demand it? Why, for instance, it is asked, should not the Indian tanners, who are gradually but surely losing their business in competition with the superior resources and energy of America, be assisted by a duty on the exports of raw skins, so that these may be retained in the country and tanned by local labour? The example of other countries is pointed to, to show how profitable the Government encouragement of local industries may be. But in all such cases there must be a rivalry, direct or implied, between the encouragement of British and Indian capital, and an Indian newspaper I have lately seen observes with caustic bitterness and no small measure of truth that, "as there can be no revival of Indian industry without some displacement of British industry, we understand the difficulty of ruling India for the good of the people of India." This is in fact one of the most hopeless aspects in which the problem before us can be considered. In the great industrial conflict of the world, England is engaged in a life struggle against American and Continental competition, and against competition also with her Colonies, and our own capitalists are keenly conscious of the fact that they are more and more dependent on their success in exploiting the vast population and natural resources of India to their own benefit. It is their aim to have a complete command of these through the importation of British capital into the country. The Government of Great Britain is identified with this policy ; and, whatever may be possible in other directions of fiscal enterprise, this at least is certain, that, having regard to the economic revolution through which India has passed, no attempt can be made to encourage Indian industries or the investment of Indian capital by means of protective legislation without a complete reversal of British policy and the sacrifice of the profits and aspirations of British capitalists.

It follows from these considerations that any proposal for a customs union between Great Britain and our self-governing Colonies can have very little application to India, and it was inevitable that the only debate in Parliament on the subject,[1] which was introduced by the late Lord Northbrook, and continued by three noble lords who had also held the office of Governor-General in India, should have proceeded on unreal and academic lines. It was indeed suggested in that discussion that we could not refuse to India the power of protection which was exercised in the self-governing Colonies, and that as the resources of revenue in India were limited, there would be a natural desire to have recourse to import duties. Such a suggestion was a mere *ballon d'essai.* A desire for protection exists, no doubt, among the people ; but it is equally certain that no proposal in this direction has been considered or ever will be seriously considered by the Indian Government. India is not yet a self-governing dependency, and its tariff policy, as Lord Elgin once declared from his place in Council, is determined by the mandate of the Secretary of State. Any proposals for fiscal protection in India—such as those which are in practice in

[1] On the 10th July 1903.

the Colonies—may be "economically inexpedient and politically dangerous," or they may "supply the party of agitation with a real grievance and with the materials for an indictment to which no reply is possible"; but this at least is known to all—that no Government at home would venture or dream of venturing to authorise the Government of India to impose any form of protective tariff against the manufacturers of the United Kingdom. In regard to preference, it is enough to say that the absence of a corresponding proportionate benefit to a country to which preferential treatment is proposed is fatal to its acceptance; and if no offer from the Colonies could compensate England for a tax on food, the case is very much stronger as regards India, for which neither Mr Chamberlain nor any of his supporters have been able to propose a definite scheme. The utmost that could result from any scheme, as far as India is concerned, would be to give some slight and inappreciable benefit to the producers of wheat, sugar, and tobacco in that country, and to impose in other respects a tax on foreign imports, which would only have the effect of raising prices to the consumer and of disarranging the fiscal relations between India and other countries. I will not say that such a scheme, however foolish it may be, might not be enforced ; but the concession of the privilege of discretionary protection, such as the self-governing Colonies enjoy, is not at present within the purview of practical politics.

On the other hand, there is an undoubtedly growing tendency among the Indians to help themselves. In accordance with the nascent feeling of patriotism, there is already a considerable, and, it would be hardly too much to say, an overwhelming, current of public sentiment in favour of using country products in preference to foreign imports. The sentiment may be said to have always existed, but the reality of the movement in this direction is due to the partition of Bengal. After exhausting every means of constitutional agitation, the people of that province fell back on new methods, which they hoped would operate on Englishmen through their pockets, and so induce public opinion to influence the Government to pay some regard to local wishes in Bengal. The idea was an ingenious one, and was encouraged, if not suggested, by the successful experience of the Chinese in boycotting American goods in order to secure better treatment of the Chinese in the United States. The feeling had, however, been in the air for a long time, and had been freely discussed in Madras and Bombay—curiously enough, not so much in Calcutta. But it is in Calcutta that the policy of boycott was first put into practical operation. In spite of official opposition of every kind, accompanied in many cases by persecution of individuals and attempts at forcible repression, it has held its own. Large assemblies of the people have sworn on the holy Ganges water and in their temples not to deal in foreign goods. It is now merely a question of organisation and persistence. These are qualities which the Bengalees are said to lack ; but they are not deficient in a spirit of self-sacrifice when the occasion arises for its exercise. The movement is already spreading to the other Presidencies, where opinion has long been in its favour. Whether they will succeed or not remains to be seen, but I have no doubt whatever that the people of India are in earnest in this movement, and will do their utmost to maintain it. Although its effect on the Manchester market has proved to be comparatively slight at present, there is more in the agitation than the Manchester merchants are willing to admit. It is in its infancy, and is in need of capital to back it. But the spread of the cotton-mill industry in Bombay, which is mostly financed by Parsi gentlemen, affords some evidence of the willingness of Indian capitalists to launch their money in commercial enterprise. The Swadeshi movement has given a vigorous fillip to this industry. New mills, floated with Indian capital, are being started in Bengal. Hand-looms have been revived. In all directions there is development of industrial investment. Indian capital is being laid out in many places on a small scale on the manufacture of materials such as glass, hardware, soap, paper, ink, matches, cutlery, and the like. A Bengal Technical Institute has been established. There are Technical Institutes in Bombay, in Ahmedabad and in Baroda. Scholarships have been endowed, and young men are pouring into the West and into Japan to equip themselves for technical industry. A Jubilee Art Academy has been started in Calcutta. A great stimulus was given by Lord Curzon to the restoration of Indian art by the establishment of the Art Exhibition which was held during the Durbar at Delhi. Industrial exhibitions are now annually held in connection with the meetings of the Indian National Congress. A scheme has lately been launched by some of the leading landholders in Bengal for an extensive store of indigenous art and industrial products in Calcutta on joint-stock principles.

Above all, there are the great schemes of that Indian millionaire and philanthropist, the late Mr Jamsetji N. Tata, of Bombay. The endowment of an Indian Institution of Research and Science at a cost of £200,000—which, I am glad to say, has been liberally supplemented by the Government of India and by the enlightened Government of Mysore—was designed to deal with the widest range of practical studies which are capable of treatment by scientific methods. This has been somewhat shorn of its original scope, and has been reduced, for a time at least, to proposals in connection with the experimental sciences of chemistry, physics, and biology. In any case, it is a grand conception. The same Indian capitalist has put forward a project for the exploitation of iron and copper mines in Central India, which, if it succeeds, will inaugurate a new era in the industrial history of India.

We have, I hope, entered upon times which offer a better prospect of attainment of the great object we have in view. Sir William Ramsay, who went out to India to report on Mr Tata's scheme, was impressed with two facts: first, that most of the population supports itself by agriculture, and that the relative proportion of manufacture to agriculture was insignificant; and second, that the raw products of India have either not been exploited or are in the hands of English companies, or are exported in an unmanufactured state. In these words Professor Ramsay sums up what I have been endeavouring to emphasise: our object must be to establish indigenous industries dealing with raw products in the country. An excellent address was delivered on this subject by His Highness the Gaekwar of Baroda on the occasion of the opening of the Industrial Exhibition at Ahmedabad. In inspiring accents he called upon his fellow-countrymen to think, to act, "to encourage and assist the commercial development of the country, and so put it on the only possible road to progress, opulence, and prosperity." For the first time a great Indian Prince has had the courage to deliver himself of such weighty sentiments, and the stimulus of his enthusiasm cannot fail to rouse the energy and practical instincts of his countrymen. The difficulties are immense, and the essential difficulty always hinges on the absolute dependence of India on Great Britain. But I have confidence in the enterprise and persistence of the people of India, among whom the seeds of a liberal education have been firmly planted. The first steps of the movement have been taken. The beginnings are small—very small at present; but, like the little cloud no bigger than a man's hand, they may grow and swell with a full promise of abundance. It rests with those who are most in sympathy with the movement, with the great body of the Indian educated community, with Englishmen who have the welfare of India at heart, to see that the present impetus does not flag, that the action taken is sustained, and that the rising interest in the subject does not dissipate itself in idle words.

ADMINISTRATIVE REFORM—I

THE SUBSTITUTION OF INDIAN FOR EUROPEAN OFFICIAL AGENCY

THE keynote of administrative reform is the gradual substitution of Indian for European official agency. This is the one end towards which the educated Indians are concentrating their efforts ; the concession of this demand is the only way by which we can make any pretence of satisfying even the most moderate of their legitimate aspirations. It is the first and most pressing duty the Government is called on to discharge.

It is necessary as an economic measure. But it is necessary also on higher grounds than those of economy. I, indeed, am not a man to depreciate the administrative qualities of my own countrymen. In the words of Lord Lytton, I may say that "I speak of what I know by my own experience, and have seen with my own eyes. No body of men in the world ever conferred more splendid benefits upon any community." I have not hesitated to dwell upon their defects, but I am not blind to their merits. I have seen too much, been too long brought into contact with the admirable work done by my predecessors and colleagues, to feel any doubt of the energy, probity, and sincerity of our young English magistrates, or of the zeal with which they devote themselves to the public service. But from the essential circumstances of the case, due to the constitution of a foreign government and alien administration, the British officials labour under disqualifications for which the general excellence of their work can afford no compensation. It is apparent that, while Indians of mature age will work for less pay than youthful Europeans, their knowledge of the language and customs of the country gives them in other respects an immense advantage. Natives of India do not require to take long furloughs to Europe to recruit their strength; their thoughts are not unceasingly distracted by interests and associations wholly foreign to their country and the work in hand; they have, of necessity, a more perfect insight into the character and conduct of the people. However great the merits of European officers may be, they can never be so great as to counterbalance advantages like these.[1] The superiority of the natives of the country in administering law and justice to their own people is indeed a fact that cannot be seriously disputed. Many Indian gentlemen may be enumerated, who have sat as judges in the High Court, whose intellectual attainments and high moral virtues sufficiently vindicate the competence of their countrymen to exercise the most responsible judicial functions. At the same time, the judicial appointments in

[1] "Few worse governments can be devised than one in which the governors are launched into office at an immature age; and when years and practice have refined their judgment and qualified them for their task, they make way for others to renew the same process—make their mistakes, learn wisdom, and spend the wisdom acquired in an idle and objectless existence in another sphere, or, in the best contingency, not in the service of those at whose expense they have acquired it. The constant change of governors and their unripeness are ever-recurring topics of remark in the discussion on our Government; and I find the judgment of an acute and not unfriendly native statesman is to the effect that in the inability to settle in India lies the most insuperable objection to our rule.

"He (Sir Salar Jung) thought, speaking of the great animosity against us, that the answer might partly be found in this—viz. 'that none of our predecessors ever were so utterly foreign to the country as we are; that with all their faults they settled among and amalgamated themselves with the people, which we, with all our virtues, could never do. This, he seems to think, is the most insuperable of all the objections against our rule.'" (*East Indian Systems of Government*, p. 73. Quoted from Dr Congreve's pamphlet on *India*, published in 1857, and reprinted in 1872.)

the lower grades of the service are already filled by Indians, and there is abundant testimony to show that they discharge their duties with integrity and ability. No authority on this subject could be higher than that of a late Lord Chancellor, the Earl of Selborne, who testified as follows[1] from his place in Parliament :—

> My lords, for some years I practised in Indian cases before the Judicial Committee of the Privy Council, and during those years there were few cases of any imperial importance in which I was not concerned. I had considerable opportunities of observing the manner in which, in civil cases, the native judges did their duty, and I have no hesitation in saying—and I know this was also the opinion of the judges during that time—that the judgments of the native judges bore most favourable comparison, as a general rule, with the judgments of the English judges. I should be sorry to say anything in disparagement of English judges, who, as a class, are most anxious carefully to discharge their duty; but I repeat that I have no hesitation in saying that in every instance, in respect of integrity, of learning, of knowledge, of the soundness and satisfactory character of the judgments arrived at, the native judgments were quite as good as those of English judges.

In the highest departments of the judicial service, as well as in the lowest, the employment of Indians is admitted to be a successful experi-

[1] As reported in the *Times*, 10th April 1883.

ment. The principle, therefore, has already been accepted : yet if any proposal be made to go further, to appoint Indians to the higher executive as well as to judicial offices, to appoint Indian district officers as well as Indian civil judges, it is greeted with an outcry of disapprobation. When recommendations are made for appointing Indians to judicial posts, there seems to be an idea underlying the proposal that this branch of the service chiefly demands those intellectual qualities in which Indians excel ; whereas the executive branch demands qualities other than intellectual, such as energy, decision, self-reliance, power of combination and organisation, of managing men, and so forth, which are deemed to be qualities as yet imperfectly developed in the Indian races. Therefore it seems to be thought better to refrain from placing Indians in the higher class of executive posts, which, according to this view, ought to be reserved almost exclusively for Europeans. This is a fair statement of the argument of persons opposed to any reform in the present system. The natives of India are assumed to be unfit to have charge of districts ; it is convenient to assume that all Englishmen are cool and wise in danger, while no natives are so, and that consequently only Englishmen, and no

Indians, are competent to be trusted with independent charge. By a process of the grossest self-adulation, we persuade ourselves to believe that natives are only useful as ministerial servants, but that the work of a district, if it is to be done at all, demands the supervision of an English officer. The truth, however, is that the Indians, as of course they must be, are the backbone of our administration. The burden and heat of the day are already borne by Indian subordinates, and in the event (as occasionally must be the case) of an incompetent European being in charge of a district, the whole of the work is done by his Indian deputies and clerks.

It is, moreover, expedient that the accession of Indian officials to the ranks of the executive service should be encouraged, even at the cost of some temporary inefficiency of administration. The argument is frequently put forward that any departure from the existing system would be followed by deterioration of efficiency. That is possible : it is even probable that there might be deterioration in the first instance ; but administrative efficiency cannot always be the sole test of policy. The argument would lead to, and is intended to lead to, the conclusion that Indians should be excluded from any participation in the Government for many years to come. There could be only one result from the acceptance of this conclusion—the indefinite prolongation and intensification of the present feeling of discontent.

Lord Ripon justly urged on behalf of his scheme of local self-government, that it would be an instrument of political education.[1] "At the outset the Governor-General in Council must explain that in advocating an extension of local self-government, and the adoption of this principle in the management of many local affairs, he does not suppose that the work will be, in the first instance, better done than if it remained in the sole hands of the Government district officers. It is not primarily with a view to improvement in administration that this measure is put forward and supported; it is chiefly desirable as an instrument of popular political education. His Excellency in Council has himself no doubt that, as local knowledge and interest are brought to bear more fully upon local administration, improved efficiency will in fact follow. But at starting there will doubtless be many failures calculated to discourage exaggerated hopes, and even in some cases to cast apparent discredit upon the principle of self-

[1] Paragraph 5 of a resolution published by the Government of India in May 1882.

government itself." These remarks have been sneered at as sentimental and ill-judged rhetoric; they seem to me to be the utterance of sound statesmanship.

It may be as truly said, that if we desire to eventually establish an independent government, we can only do so by training the people to a sense of self-help and self-reliance through familiarity with the details of executive work. We are told that before entrusting the Indians with power we must devote our energies to educating them in character and common-sense. But it is only by the actual exercise of power that men acquire a sense of responsibility in the use of it. How can we expect progress in the development of national character when we only employ a comparatively feeble implement to improve, and at the same time apply a powerful engine to deteriorate? A system of government which deliberately excludes the people from power is more efficacious in depressing their character than all our laws and school-books can be in elevating it. However great may be the energy and activity of British officials in India, however thorough may be their administrative efficiency, it counts as dross if they lack the higher genius of training the people by making them work for themselves, of evoking their powers by affording them opportunities for their exercise, and of raising them from a condition of mere passive subjection to a capacity for the discharge of higher responsibilities. A nation is the best administered which can manage its own concerns with the least departmental interference, and no system of government can be progressive or beneficial which does not foster the self-reliance of the people and encourage their aspirations to realise their destiny through their own exertions. It was one of Mr Gladstone's most famous sayings, that it is liberty alone which fits men for liberty.

It may be added that as judicial functions are superior to administrative duties, so it is important that the powers of the administrator should be entrusted to natives of India before those of the judge. I am careful to affirm the necessity of keeping in the hands of the judiciary the power of check and control, revision and appeal ; and this may be used as an argument in favour of the cautious delegation of judicial authority to Indians ; but there is no corresponding reason why all the real business of administration should be retained in the hands of Englishmen. On the contrary, it is desirable that, during the period of transition upon which we are now fairly launched, the English Government should at every possible opportunity invest Indian officials with executive duties, and so educate them onwards to undertake higher responsibilities. The gradual withdrawal of our interference in Indian affairs should rather be marked by our systematic resignation of executive functions than by the relinquishment of judicial appointments which carry with them the right of appellate and revisional jurisdiction.

A worldly-wise policy would also induce the Government to entrust executive duties to Indian hands. The existing system of administration presents the somewhat anomalous appearance of executive work done by officials of the ruling race, while the natives of the country sit in judgment on the work so done, and naturally subject it to free and often hostile criticism. Great friction is occasionally caused by the exercise of this right of criticism ; and although, on the whole, its influence is beneficial, it cannot be denied that it is one of the means which serve to alienate British officialism and the Indian public. How obvious seems the suggestion to transfer the duties which excite so much animadversion from Europeans to Indians, and to leave the Indian press to sit as a tribunal over the official peccadilloes, not of Englishmen, but of its own countrymen !

Indian Official Agency

This aspect of the case is well considered in a pamphlet which was published in Calcutta by the late Sir Henry Harrison, an eminent member of the Civil Service. He wrote :—

The Indian community, in tastes, in interests, in intellectual attainments, in desire for progress, is broken up into countless divisions and subdivisions; and as soon as its members are entrusted with the powers and responsibilities of administration, all these diversities and rivalries at once come to the surface. Politically, the true *rôle* of Englishmen in the India of the future should be that of arbitrators between rival sections and interests of the native community—a *rôle* which by their natural qualities they are well qualified to discharge. Who that has any experience of dealing with native gentlemen charged with administrative functions has not seen numerous occasions on which the opinions of one or two Europeans present are eagerly sought for, and allowed to turn the scale at once between contending parties? As the natives of India gain a larger and larger share in the administrative work of the country, the fire of criticism, which is now concentrated on the European functionaries, will be directed against one another, and they will fall into groups and parties as numerous as are the separate interests involved, all of which may, if wisely handled, be permeated by a common devotion to a common country.

Repress educated natives, distrust them, let them see that the policy of India for the Indians and of training them to administer their own country is a fiction, and you weld them all into one solid phalanx, united by the common bond of despair and hatred towards Europeans. Can any policy be more insensate than this? But open the door to their ambitions, and you at once let in all the emulations, class interests, sectional friction, which if not in themselves good, are at any rate a necessary element in a healthy state of society, and instead of a solid phalanx you have a crowd of aspirants competing with one another under conditions which the Government will prescribe, and in a race of which it will be the umpire and the distributor of the prizes.

These excellent observations afford, I conceive, the strongest common-sense argument in favour of the delegation of executive and administrative authority into Indian hands. It is necessary to do so on grounds of economy, it is necessary as a concession to the reasonable and natural aspirations of the natives of the country, and it is no less necessary from a common-sense point of view, in furtherance of a wise and harmonious administration.

I am compelled to add that under the Government of Lord Curzon there was a regrettable reaction in this direction as well as in others. The merits of Lord Curzon's rule were many. He displayed indefatigable energy in grappling with the details of administration. He never spared himself in his efforts to become personally acquainted with all corners of the Empire. I yield to no one in my admiration for his talents, culture, imagination, and unswerving purpose. I respect, if I do not always admire, the uncompromising manner in which he crushed out all opposition to his own policy. Especially I applaud his firm determination to put down military lawlessness and to assert the claims of justice irrespective of all racial considerations. But the higher my appreciation of Lord Curzon's ability and character, the keener is my disappointment at the measures of his Government. He showed that he could use his strength in various beneficent ways, but he lamentably failed to satisfy the expectations which had been formed of his masterful personality. He placed the seal upon a great change in our relations with the independent princes of India, who have now been relegated to the position of vassals of the Viceroy. He arrested the progress of education and set back the dial of local self-government in the metropolis of India. His confidence in the capacity of a bureaucratic administration of foreigners to solve political problems of any degree of complexity was unbounded, and amounted to a prejudice which proved most detrimental to popular and national aspirations. Centralisation was his foible and departmentalism his weakness. His desire was to govern well, but it was not to govern through the people or with their aid. It is not too much to say that he convinced himself that no official business would be efficiently transacted unless it was controlled by a department of officials with Englishmen at their head. It was in this spirit that he fell back on the policy of inquiry through commissions, which were absolutely dominated in all cases by the official element. His imperial prepossessions led him to subordinate all considerations to the advancement of British interests, openly avowing that the commercial exploitation of India by Englishmen and the administration of the country by Englishmen were aspects of the same question and of the same duty without distinction of object or purpose or aim. In the furtherance of these views he deliberately sacrificed the interests of the Indian people, and in particular refused to adopt the most urgent and simple measures for ameliorating the lot of the voiceless toilers in the tea-gardens of Assam. Above all, the trend of his policy was to exclude the children of the soil from positions of trust and responsibility, to deny them the opportunities of acquiring the qualifications necessary for their success in the posts monopolised by Englishmen, and to limit the avenues of their employment in the public service. There has been a perceptible tendency during the past few years for the Government to recruit a larger number of its well-paid officers from England ; and this tendency has been noticeable not in one department only, but in all.

ADMINISTRATIVE REFORM—II

THE SEPARATION OF JUDICIAL FROM EXECUTIVE FUNCTIONS, AND THE RE-ORGANISATION OF THE CIVIL SERVICE

ANOTHER administrative reform which has now become a burning question is the separation of the judicial from the executive service. Under existing arrangements the district magistrate is at one and the same time the head of the police and the head of the magistracy, and it is his duty to watch the police investigation of the more important cases, to instruct investigating officers, to read police reports and papers as they come in, and finally to decide whether a case should or should not be sent up for trial before himself or one of his subordinates. He is also in a position to exercise control over the trial of these cases by his subordinates. I cannot imagine that serious doubt can be felt by anyone who is acquainted with the practical administration of justice in India that the combination of executive and judicial functions in the same person does actually lead to practical abuse. It is a matter of universal knowledge that subordinate magistrates, whose position and promotion are dependent on the district magistrate, cannot, in such circumstances, discharge their judicial duties with that degrée of independence which ought to characterise a court of justice. To furnish evidence of this would be an easy task. Mr Monomohun Ghose's famous twenty cases[1] are typical of others,[2] and the

[1] *A Compilation of Cases illustrating the Evils of the Union of Judicial and Executive Functions in Bengal*, by Monomohun Ghose, barrister-at-law, 1896.

[2] The following amusing, but painfully instructive and suggestive, notes were published by the late Rai Bahadur Parbati Charan Roy, one of the most distinguished and able Indian officers in my time, after his retirement, in 1898, in illustration of the relations which existed between himself, a subordinate deputy magistrate, and Mr B., the magistrate of the district in which he was serving :—

CASE NO. 1.

Parbati Bu,—If the facts found by you are correct, the sentence passed is utterly inadequate. Government has expressly directed that when an accused person is convicted of bringing a false charge (except in exceptional circumstances) he shall be punished severely. The sentence you have passed is not more than the complainant would have received had the charge of theft been true. It should have been at least four times as much. I am very much dissatisfied at this, and so will the L. G. be if the case comes before him. What explanation have you to offer?

16.1.92. (Sd.) B.

experience of every judge, magistrate, and counsel could add to their number, but as they stand they are enough to show that mischief has resulted. It must be remembered also that a very small proportion of cases in which interference has been exercised comes to notice, for discreet officers will always keep their interference and control in the background. The fact remains that, however indirectly the power may be exercised, the union of police prosecutor and judge in the same hands leads to results which

I do not consider the sentence (six months) to be at all inadequate. I have awarded what I considered to be the proper punishment. The accused charged the complainant with the theft of a Garu (brass jug), valued at Rs. 14, for which the punishment might have been two weeks.

16.1.92. (Sd.) P. C. R.

Parbati Bu,—The sentence is utterly inadequate. If this occurs again I shall report your misconduct to Government. The tone of your remarks is also insubordinate and improper. Please clearly understand that I shall not tolerate this kind of thing for a moment.

18.1.92. (Sd.) B.

Case No. 2.

Parbati Bu,—You told me yesterday that there were reasons for the delay in this case. I find no reasons whatever on the record.

The delay from the 5th to 14th is much too long.

Why were not arguments heard on the same day?

Why was the application from the first party acceded to?

You do not seem to understand the necessity of disposing of these cases at the earliest possible date.

Very bad. (Sd.) B.

are as objectionable in practice as they are anomalous in theory.

At the same time I recognise that the nature and degree of the evil vary greatly, and that the application of a practical remedy raises problems of difficulty and complexity which do not admit of summary solution. The Government of India is complicated by the fact that the vast population over which it rules consists of elements so dissimilar as to render it impracticable to place them under any one system of administration.

CASE No. 3.

Parbati Bu,—In this case the right of cross-examination seems to have been abused. You must check this.

3.4.92. (Sd.) B.

CASE No. 4.

Parbati Bu,—This is a most inadequate and unsuitable sentence. The constable was wantonly assaulted without provocation in the discharge of his duties, and you say that the offence is not at all a serious one. Why not? The accused should have been sentenced to two months' rigorous imprisonment. Your judgment is careless and slovenly, and does not state the facts. If it were not that you were about to retire, I should hand the case up to Government as a specimen of inefficiency.

(Sd.) B.

As I have said, the injuries were slight; and considering the age (20) of the accused and the circumstance that the assault was not a premeditated one, I awarded fine, and not imprisonment.

I have no objection to the magistrate of the district handing this or any other case of mine to Government. It is not certain that I shall soon retire.

12.4.92. (Sd.) P. C. ROY.

They exhibit, to quote from the words of a well-known official report, every stage of human progress and every type of human enlightenment and superstition—from the highly educated classes represented by the gentlemen who distinguish themselves at the Universities or the Inns of Court, to the hill chieftain who a few years ago sacrificed an idiot on the top of a mountain to obtain a favourable decision in a Privy Council appeal. The natural and constant tendency is towards advance. It may be true, as Sir Frederick Halliday declared in 1856, that the Oriental idea of provincial government is to unite all powers into one centre, and that nothing can be more opposed to the Oriental plan of administration than the entire separation of judicial from executive duties. What Lord Canning wrote in 1857 was no doubt also true at a time when no Indian university had been established, and the government of the country was still carried on by the Honourable East India Company. He wrote:—

We believe that what has been called the patriarchal form of government is, in the present condition of the people of Bengal, most congenial to them and most understood by them; and as regards the governing power, the concentration of all responsibility upon one officer cannot fail to keep his attention alive and stimulate his energy in every department to the utmost, whilst it will preclude the growth of those obstructions to good administration which are apt to spring up where two co-ordinate officers divide the authority.

But there have been many changes in India since the Mutiny, and it is the province of statesmanship, while taking occasion by the hand, to make such modifications in the form of administration as the altered conditions of the country from time to time and in different localities may indicate.

The keynote of the policy which should now be followed is struck in the following remarks in a published letter from the late Lord Hobhouse, dated the 7th January 1896 :—

It has always seemed to me that the substitution of a fixed impersonal law for the personal view of the ruler for the time being, and in the particular case, is one of the most important advances in good government that can be made in any country; and again, that this advantage cannot be secured unless the law is declared by a separate staff of functionaries. How far the separation shall be carried, so as to secure the utmost amount of independence in the judiciary that is consistent with the unity and stability of government, is a question of statesmanship, depending on the condition of the country. I believe that under Asiatic rulers the principle of independence was so merged in that of unity as to be very weak, even if perceptible, and I have always claimed for our countrymen that we have either introduced it or made it a living thing. In the course of my work as Law Member of Council I held many conversations and discussions with Bengal zemindars, and with nobles and landlords in other parts of India, and, rightly or wrongly, I came to the belief that they had grasped the principle of judicial independence firmly, and put a true value upon it, and looked upon it as a great safeguard.

Lord Hobhouse had acquired his experience of India many years before, but he was able even then to perceive how firmly the idea of a reign of law based on British models of jurisprudence had been established in India by the British Government. It is the experience of nearly all competent observers since his time that this conception has grown more and more securely rooted among the people. In the face of this conception it is idle to argue any longer in favour of "the Oriental view that all power should be collected in the hands of a single official, so that the people of the district should be able to look upon one man in whom the various branches of authority are centred, and who is the visible representative of Government." It is true that this is the Oriental view, but we have deliberately destroyed it by the introduction of an Occidental system of jurisprudence. It dies hard among the official classes who proclaim it, but it has no longer any vitality except among backward communities. I doubt whether it can be said that in any other direction the contact between West and East has had any real effect in de-orientalising the Indian people. But in this direction the influence of Western thought has been allowed the fullest scope, and the idea of personal government has given way to the reign of an impersonal law.

The time has come when this condition of things should be officially recognised, and a complete separation of judicial from executive functions is imperatively called for in the advanced provinces in India. It would be desirable to introduce the separation gradually, and, in the first instance, into the most advanced portions of these provinces only. But the sooner a beginning is made the better, and it would naturally be in the metropolitan districts that the new system would be inaugurated. Our policy should be a cautious one, for it is a fatal error to make concessions which it is afterwards necessary to withdraw. Lord Hobhouse justly points out that the adoption of the new policy must depend on the condition of the country. In many parts of India it would be an act of folly to introduce any change, and in such places, whatever abuses may be inherent in the present system, there can be no doubt that the balance of advantage would be altogether in favour of leaving the existing arrangements undisturbed. The original system everywhere in India was in accord with the concentration of power in the hands of a single individual. In many parts of India which are still fitly administered on primitive lines, it will be necessary for many a long day to maintain such concentration. But India, as a whole, does not mark time, and methods which are appropriate to such tracts, and were appropriate one hundred years ago—or even fifty years ago—in Bengal, Madras, and Bombay, are no longer applicable to the advanced portions of those provinces.

It is surprising how little change there has been in the form of administration in India during the past century. The constitution of the Indian Civil Service is theoretically unchanged. It is a fine old service, and has enrolled within its ranks men of whom the mother country may well be proud. An appointment in that service implies a position of trust and influence, the exercise of power and responsibility, a capacity for good or evil altogether beyond the range of ordinary mortals in workaday life. It was organised with consummate skill by our early administrators. The arrangement of districts with a population of from one to three million inhabitants, and of an area of from two thousand to ten thousand square miles, over which a single officer presides—in whom all authority is centralised ; by whom the working of all departments is controlled and brought to a common action ; to whom the civil surgeon, the district superintendent of police, the engineer, and a large staff of assistants .and deputies exercising magisterial, executive, and revenue functions are all carefully subordinated with almost martial precision ; who is himself the hand and eye of Government ; upon whose resource, efficiency, and presence of mind may often depend the happiness of multitudes of human beings—this is indeed a vigorous and attractive administrative conception, a monument to the organising ability of those who devised it. It is, however, a form of administration adapted only to autocratic rule. It has been perceptibly dying out, from its inherent inapplicability to an environment where changes are becoming rapid. I can remember several desperate attempts to galvanise it into life,—especially by the ablest of our recent administrators, Sir George Campbell, Sir John Strachey, and Sir Charles Elliott. But they failed, as everyone must fail who tries to withstand the advancing tide.

For my part, I think that even in its executive aspect we ought to acknowledge that the government should now find expression in a form of administration more representative and less concentrated in individuals, and would point out that if subordinate executive officers were chosen more largely from permanent residents of the locality, it would obviate that habit of constant transfer and change which is the bane of the present system.

But it is in the judicial branch of the service that reorganisation is most urgently required. The members of the Civil Service, when very young and very ignorant of the language, are vested with magisterial powers beyond comparison greater than those possessed by corresponding functionaries under any civilised government, and, being uncontrolled by public opinion, and with little judicial experience, it would be strange if they were not led into occasional errors, and sometimes into abuse of power. Their faults are for the most part the faults of youth. It is the system that is to blame. It is a marked defect under our present administration that native officers are also vested with magisterial powers at too early an age.

Considerations of climate render it imperative that Englishmen should go to India while they are young, but there can be no excuse for the appointment of natives of the country as magistrates at an unripe age. Yet this is almost invariably done, and there is a rule that no Indian who is not already in Government service shall be eligible for the appointment of deputy magistrate if he is above the age of twenty-five years. In this respect, it seems that we are blinded by the false analogy of the Civil Service, which is a body of foreigners, the defects of whose organisation should be corrected and not copied when officers who are not foreigners are concerned. There is no reason why, over the greater part of India, important judicial functions should any longer be discharged by persons of immature years, and it is a crying reform in regard to the administration of justice (in all but backward tracts, where the patriarchal system must still prevail) that only those persons should be vested with judicial powers whose age, training, and experience afford a guarantee for the proper exercise of authority.

The remedy lies in the complete separation of the judicial from the executive service. The Indian Civil Service should be recruited for executive offices only, and judicial appointments should be reserved, as they are in other countries, for members of the legal profession, who are trained to undertake the duties attaching to them. In no other way would the separation be really complete, and by no other process of selection is it possible to secure the proper discharge of judicial functions. The whole training of a civilian in India unfits him for judicial work. Patience and discrimination, respect for the forms of the law, rigid imperviousness to rumour and to outside report—these are some of the qualifications which are the essential attributes of the judicial office. There is no stage in the career of a civilian which affords him the opportunity for their acquisition. It is not surprising that we should find "executive judges" among the judiciary, when we see that young civilians are taken straight from the Financial Department or the Settlement Camp and placed upon the bench. The civilian judge has never had a proper grounding in law, and he never knows up to the day of his appointment whether he is to be a judicial officer. But his training has been all along on executive lines. He can say, like Horace's sarcastic god :—

> Olim truncus eram ficulnus, inutile lignum,
> Cum faber incertus scamnum faceretne Priapum,
> Maluit esse deum, deus inde ego!

I have seen a High Court judge promoted to be a Chief Commissioner and another to be Foreign Secretary ; and the promotion of High Court and Chief Court judges to be members of the Executive Council, and even Lieutenant-Governors of provinces, is still not an uncommon spectacle. This I mention as typical of another abuse which will never be cured so long as the judiciary is chosen from the ranks of the Civil Service. The judiciary ought to be subordinate to the highest judicial authority, and there ought to be no promotion from judicial to executive posts, or *vice versâ*. There can be no real independence on the part of the judicial service so long as judges are dependent for promotion and transfer on the will of the executive government. I do not say that the power of transfer is now abused, but it is certainly open to abuse. It is an essential feature, therefore, of the scheme for the separation of executive and judicial functions that subordinate judicial officers, of whatever grade, should be placed under the control and orders of the High Court.

There is another grave hardship which can only be remedied by the appointment of magistrates who have no concern whatever with executive work. It is a great practical grievance among persons whose misfortune takes them into court that the magistrate who tries their case may, for all they know, fix the hearing of it in camp. Magistrates who are executive officers, and especially magistrates who are in executive charge of subdivisions, are required to spend a considerable portion of the year on tour. It may readily be imagined how parties are harassed by such an arrangement. Apart from personal inconvenience, they are put to the greatest difficulty in obtaining legal advice and assistance away from headquarters.

The executive and judicial hierarchies should be completely distinct from one another. The whole of the executive administration should be in the hands of the Indian Civil Service. The executive head of the district should no longer be described as a district magistrate ; he should be designated as district officer or deputy commissioner of the district. In his hands should rest the entire control over the police, and the responsibility for all branches of the revenue administration. He should be the controlling authority over municipalities and local boards, and would still be, as he is now, the hand and eye of the executive government in his district. But neither the district officer nor any officer subordinate to him should exercise judicial functions. Under this scheme it would be possible to get rid of the superior police service, thus effecting a substantial economy, while at the same time simplifying the administration. I would not listen for a moment to the argument that this rearrangement would result in a loss of prestige to the district officer. If at present he derives any prestige from his power of interference with judicial work, it is desirable that this stumbling-block should be removed from his way. But I deny that his prestige would suffer, and consider that his position as executive head of the district, especially as direct head of the police, would rather endow him with increased influence and give him ample authority. While full executive power would thus rest with the civilian district officer, the whole of the judicial administration of the district would be under the district and sessions judge, who would be directly subordinate to the High Court. To preside over the local courts there would be, as now, the district and session judge, subordinate judges, magistrates, and munsifs. But appointments to all these offices would be made by the High Court, and the selection would be made from among advocates and pleaders and other members of the legal profession. Very highly qualified material is available for the purpose. There are many experienced English barristers now in India who would make admirable judges, and discharge the duties far better that the average civilian. Gradually, no doubt, the number of Indian judicial officers would increase, and this result I would welcome in the interests of both efficiency and economy.

These proposals contemplate a reduction in the rate of recruitment for the Indian Civil Service, and it is to be regretted that the practice has been adhered to of recruiting for this service exclusively on actuarial principles, without regard to changes of constitution which sooner or later are inevitable. The excessive recruitment of recent years has rendered it difficult to give practical effect on an early date to any reform. A large phalanx of junior civilians remains, and will for some time remain, who have to be provided for in the higher judicial as well as in executive posts, and they have claims and rights which it is not possible to disregard. But in calculating for future recruitments we should be prepared to exclude judicial appointments in increasing number from the cadre of the service.

In any case the Indian Civil Service as at present constituted is doomed. It is a form of administration both bureaucratic and autocratic, and is an organisation suited only to a government of foreigners. It will pass away after a prolonged period of magnificent work, to be replaced by a more popular system which shall perpetuate its efficiency while avoiding its defects. Representation in the English sense of election by vote is not so much what is wanted as the selection of representative members of the community who will possess the highest possible qualifications for the discharge of local duties. The principles of administration for which we are indebted to Lord Ripon have paved the way for this reform, and centralisation is already giving way to local self-government. In the natural course of things administrative officers will be chosen more and more from the permanent residents of the locality. The interests of the public service and of the community concerned will alike be served by the appointment of an indigenous agency on the spot to perform functions for which we now import foreigners from Europe, and Indians brought from every other part of the province than that in which they are employed.

ADMINISTRATIVE REFORM—III

LOCAL SELF-GOVERNMENT AND THE LEGISLATIVE COUNCILS

THE people of India possess an instinctive capacity for local self-government which centuries of misrule have not eradicated. The inhabitants of an Indian village under their own princes formed a sort of petty republic, the affairs of which were managed by hereditary officers, any unfit person being set aside by popular judgment in favour of a more acceptable member of his family. It is by reason of the British administration only that the popular authority of the village headman has been sapped, that the responsibility of the village accountant and record-keeper has been destroyed, and the judicial powers of the Punchayet, or Committee of Five, subverted. A costly and mechanical centralisation took the place of a system of local self-government and local arbitration. The old order can, of course, never be restored in its integrity, but the development of local institutions which Lord Ripon's policy inaugurated was designed to reconcile if possible the traditional forms of a native authority with the wants of a modern civilisation. It was a decisive advance in the right direction, of delegating the administration of local affairs to local bodies, who, however inferior they may be to the district officers in knowledge of the principles of administration, have the compensating advantage of a far more direct interest in the result. The administration has been localised, and the trading, manufacturing, and banking classes, no less than the agricultural, have been endowed again with corporate life.

As it is the development of local independence and self-government which, more than anything else, has given stability to the political institutions of England, so it is by a system of localised administration that we may hope for improvement and stability in the political institutions of India. We have sown throughout the Empire the seeds of representative government, and it remains to foster their growth. It is not only in the direction of land administration that I deprecate a policy of bureaucratic interference. Speaking generally on this subject of State intervention, I will say that the proper procedure is to wait, and in the most conservative spirit watch over and encourage indigenous effort, to restore life from within, to infuse in this way confidence among the people, and then to build up a political order upon existing foundations, which shall eventually be able to stand by itself with increasing firmness. These remarks are of easy application to particular cases, but especially they apply to the local self-government laws which have been passed by Government. The extension of local self-government was not wisely initiated in all cases. The extension ought to have been made gradually, to selected areas first, and afterwards to others, but in all cases with perfect confidence and in an ungrudging spirit. To enforce the principle wholesale in all places, and then to impose on it close and intolerable restrictions, was to court its failure. I would not be understood to imply that failure has followed; far from it! It is sufficient to say that the success of Lord Ripon's scheme was generously and fully acknowledged by Lord Elgin; but it has succeeded in spite of the conditions with which it was unwisely fettered. Freedom from official tutelage is essential to healthy and independent growth. This principle cannot be enunciated too often or too distinctly, and it is the more necessary to dwell upon it as, from the nature of the case, its application is very repugnant to the rising, ambitious, and energetic advisers of Government.

To officials zealous for improvement, it is trying to see important schemes, calculated to confer great benefit on a large community, postponed or marred from ignorance, or apathy, or indifference. But patience is necessary in the conduct of all public affairs, and those whose favourite projects are thwarted and opposed should remember that the establishment, development, and practical working of self-government is not only an end to be pursued, but a great object of political education to be attained. It is better that even useful reforms should be postponed for a time, and ultimately carried out with the consent of local bodies, and in the form most acceptable to them, than that they should be enforced at once, with a disregard of the feelings of the local body. We should respect the independence of such bodies; we should retain sufficient control over them to see that they do not permanently, obstinately, or slothfully neglect their duty towards their fellow-citizens; but having planted this small tree of self-government, we ought not always to be pulling it up to look at its roots in order to see how far they have got down into the ground. It is hopeless to expect any real development of local self-government if local bodies are subjected to check and interference in matters of detail. The assistance and support of Government should be given—in Lord Ripon's words —"in the manner best calculated to preserve the Commissioners' freedom of action within the limits of their attributions, and not to weaken their sense of self-reliance."

In order to give real responsibility to local boards and municipalities, they should be so constituted as to be free from the domination of the local officials. It was Lord Ripon's desire that the necessary control should be exercised from without rather than from within, and that the chairman should, as a rule, and wherever practicable, be a non-official person. But in district boards the chairman is invariably the district officer, and there is a growing tendency to appoint that officer to be chairman of the local municipality. The influence of the Government representative is, however, so great that it is rarely possible for the local commissioners to arrive at an independent decision in the presence of the district officer, and the consequence has been that the educative value of local administrative bodies has been greatly impaired. It is found that, in practice, the official chairman not only takes the lead but concentrates the whole of the administrative management in his own hands. If, therefore, local self-government is to play the part which properly belongs to it, of training the people in the management of public affairs, the procedure recommended by Lord Ripon should be revived. The risk of failure in efficiency which must be run is altogether incommensurate with the value of the boon of political education simultaneously at a great number of centres.

Some change is also called for in the elective constitution of these bodies. The introduction of the elective system has proved a practical obstacle to the success of local self-government in India. It has proved on occasions to be the source of racial and religious quarrel. It is a practical difficulty in the way of providing adequate representation of minorities, such as Mahomedans, for instance ; a difficulty which exists in a greater degree in India than in most other countries. But the fundamental objection to the system of election arises from its incompatibility with the Indian conception of personal dignity. There is an intense dislike to the humiliation of canvassing, and the best men are reluctant to put themselves in competition with a candidate whom they consider socially inferior to themselves. It is well not to forget that popular institutions in Europe, and especially in England, have usually had their origin in aristocratic and oligarchic privileges, and it is not unreasonable that India, which is and always has been an aristocratic and conservative country, should also pass through this phase. If we honestly wish to associate the people of India with the government of their country, we ought to begin with the extension of their liberties upon lines which are most likely to succeed. The recognition of the aristocratic principle in Indian society would be a decisive step towards making the local bodies genuinely representative. A law reconstituting those bodies in accordance with this suggestion would have to be sufficiently elastic to cover the diversity of conditions existing in different parts of India, but for the present purpose it is enough to say that birth, as well as election and nomination by Government, should be recognised as a principle of selection.[1]

The greatest of the administrative reforms which has been effected in India since Lord

[1] I acknowledge with pleasure the powerful support of these views and of other suggestions for extending local self-government in India contained in the special article on Indian affairs in the *Times* of 20th August 1906.

Ripon's time is the reconstitution of the Provincial Legislative Councils on a representative basis. No measure was ever more amply discussed or more urgently pressed upon the Government by the insistence of popular opinion. After seven years of preparation and consideration the law was passed, and a memorable step was taken, for which the educated Indian public will always be grateful as a concession to their just demands. It was not an adequate concession, but it was a great and decisive recognition of their claim to some independent representation in the councils of Government. In these eloquent words Mr Gladstone described the effect which had been produced on his mind by this measure for enlarging the liberties of the Indian people:—

I believe we are justified in looking forward not merely to a nominal but to a real living representation of the people of India. The great nation to which we belong has undoubtedly had to do most difficult tasks in the government and in the foundation of the institutions of extraneous territories. But all the other parts of the British Empire have presented to us a simple problem in comparison with the great problem presented to us by India. Its magnitude, its peculiarity, is such that the task of Great Britain in this respect is far greater than that which any other country has attempted, and far greater than that which it has itself attempted beyond the sea in any of the dependencies of the Empire. I rejoice to think that a great and real advance has been made both before and especially since the direct transfer of the Indian Government to the immediate superintendence of the executive at home and to the authority of the Imperial legislature. The progress thus made has been effected by the constant application to the Government of India of the minds of able men acting under a strong sense of political responsibility. All these things induce us to look forward cheerfully to a great future for India, and to expect that a real success will attend the genuine application, even though it may be a limited one, of the elective principle to the government of that vast and almost immeasurable community. If this attempt be successful, it will be the accomplishment of a task to which it would be difficult to find a parallel in history.

This reform dates from 1892. I was a member of a Provincial Legislative Council for some years before the change was made and for some years afterwards, and am therefore in a favourable position to judge of its operation. Not only was the constitution of the Councils changed, but their functions also were modified to some extent. The right of interpellation and of calling for papers was allowed, and the right of exercising some financial control was admitted. These privileges have not been abused. On the contrary, the provisions of the new law have operated to the general satisfaction of the public, and to the advantage of the Government. The Indian Councils Act has worked well; but it was not a perfect measure, and it labours under defects on the surface which no amount of tactfulness or happy give-and-take on the part of provincial governors or elected members can obviate.

While I am writing, the Executive Council of the Government of India is deliberating on proposed reforms in the constitution of the Legislative Council of the Governor-General. It is understood that the changes contemplated relate to three points only. The first is the very limited amount of time—viz., one day—given to the discussion of the Budget; the second is the question of moving amendments; the third and most important is the extension of the representative element. All three are very desirable reforms, and they stand in the fore-front of the political programme of the National Congress. The Viceroy's Legislative Council consists of twenty-five members, of whom only five are elected—one by the Chamber of Commerce of Calcutta, and the other four by four provinces. The demand of the Congress is that the proportion of elected members should be raised to twelve, of whom ten should be assigned to different provinces. It is proposed also that the right of members to move amendments should be confined to one amendment each. These are most moderate proposals, and it may be expected that they will be acceded to.

But these modifications in the constitution of the Governor-General's Council, necessary as they are, will do little more than touch the fringe of the reform now called for. It is in the Provincial Legislative Councils that the legislation most directly affecting the interests of the people is carried out, and what is urgently required is the reorganisation of the Provincial Councils.

It is impossible to give adequate representation to a province containing many millions of inhabitants in a Council of only twenty members. But the number of Provincial Councillors is limited under the present law to twenty. It is necessary, therefore, to enlarge these Councils. It is expedient also, in order to secure their stability and dignity, to provide a certain *ex-officio* qualification for membership. This *ex-officio* element should consist not of officials only, but also of noblemen whose position and status in the country entitle them to be recognised as legislators. The Provincial Legislative Council should comprise the principal Indian dignitaries in the province ; and as it is advisable to draw a precise line, it may be said that all Maharajah Bahadurs, Maharajahs, and Nawab Bahadurs, as well as all Indian gentlemen who have been honoured with the decoration of Knight Commander of the Star of India, or Knight Commander of the Indian Empire, should be *ex-officio* life members. Such recognition is due to their rank, to their stake in the country, to the respect in which they are held by the people, and to the influence they exercise. It is desirable on all grounds to encourage them to take an active part in the administration of public business. They take little or no part at present ; but their inclusion in Council and their participation in legislation and the affairs of State would immensely strengthen the hands of Government. All who have thought on the subject have felt the wisdom of some such provision as this ; and it has been suggested, considering the present limited number of councillors, that the noblemen of the province should be invited to elect a member from among themselves. Such a proposal is, however, not only inadequate, but it would be distasteful to their sentiment and lowering to their prestige. The difficulty cannot be met except by a proportionate increase of the numbers of the

Council. The official members should be limited to ten, and the nobility, though the number would vary in different provinces, would not ordinarily exceed fifteen life-members. The political instincts of these noblemen would furnish the necessary counterpoise, if any is needed, to the large infusion of middle-class representation which every system of election must introduce.

It would be left, as it is now, to the elected members to constitute what may be called the "opposition." The electoral bodies would continue to be the District Boards and Municipalities, the Presidency Corporations, the Chambers of Commerce and Trade, and the Universities. It would be reasonable to allow thirty members for the representation of such bodies. There should be one elected member for each district or administrative unit. The Council would then be supplemented by Government nominees, selected to represent official interests and other sections of the community—such as the European, Mahomedan, or Parsee—which might not otherwise be sufficiently provided for. This right of nomination is necessary for several reasons :—in order that the Government itself may be fully represented ; in order that a fair representation of minorities may be secured ; and (although in less degree) in order that individual members who are truly representative and worthy to serve on the Council, but who, for some cause or other, have not been elected, or it may be have not stood for election, may be appointed. I would fix the limit of Government nominees at fifteen, or one-half of the number of elected members.

The whole Council would then consist of about seventy members. The members would vary with the size of the different provinces, and the figures I have given are suitable to the requirements of the largest province. If this number appears large in comparison with the present number, it must be admitted that it is not large when compared with the area and population of the provinces, or with the constitution of representative chambers in other countries. There is a prejudice against a large Council on the ground that numbers will create confusion and hinder the despatch of work. But in this matter we have experience to guide us, and no objection to a large Council will be found to derive any support from the proceedings of the Presidency Corporations, or of the Senate of the Universities. I have always found in my own observation that the larger the meeting the greater is the common-sense of the assembly, the sounder is the decision arrived at, and the more amenable the whole gathering is to the influence of authority. The varying and conflicting interests of those concerned, the respect for duly constituted authority which is inherent in Orientals, and their desire to stand well with Government, are considerations which effectually restrain them from identifying themselves as a body with any factious opposition. In an enlarged Council the Government would run no risk of defeat. It is only by the adoption of such a scheme that the Councils can be established on a really representative basis. Its adoption would not only afford satisfaction to the educated classes of the community, but it would gratify and conciliate the nobility, and secure for the conservative and aristocratic elements of the country a share in the responsibilities of empire commensurate to their rank. Far from impairing the executive administration, it would prove to be a source of strength in all measures for the welfare of the people.

ENGLAND AND INDIA

It should be a source of unfeigned satisfaction to persons interested in India when closer attention is given in England to Indian affairs. This closer attention exercises a valuable influence: our own moral sense is awakened by increased knowledge; more adequate knowledge of actual facts is accompanied by a livelier consciousness of deficiency and of increased responsibility. On the other hand, our Indian fellow-subjects are clear gainers from the stimulus which their rulers receive from the beneficial action of public opinion in Europe.

I am not disposed to overrate the value of such influence, and I am free to admit that the most active manifestations of English opinion have often been actuated by race animosity. But even in such cases English opinion is able to exercise a beneficial influence in comparison with Anglo-Indian opinion in India. It finds utterance in more temperate and decorous language. No vulgar abuse of Indians,[1] such as sometimes sweeps over India, would be tolerated in this country. The occasional outbursts in the yellow press, deplorable as they are, do not affect the general truth of this statement. Distance from the scene enables men to judge of events with less excitement and irritability. There could be no more healthy symptom than the adherence of the Labour party and of the

[1] In order that my readers may be able to form some idea of the language which Anglo-Indian journals have not been ashamed to use, I give below an extract from a newspaper which appeared at a time when the Ilbert Bill agitation may be supposed to have died out:—

"Baboo Lal Mohun Ghosh has decided to accept the invitation of the Deptford 400 to become the Liberal candidate for the representation of their new borough. It is not too much to say that this rabid, worthless mob of four hundred is more fit for the inside of a lunatic asylum than for catering for the political well-being of our native land. If a Bengalee Baboo can enter Parliament, it will soon become a favourite resort for Aryans. In an insensate, idiotic thirst for novelty, where will an English mob stop? Could a chimpanzee be trained to stand for a borough, doubtless he would be found to have an excellent chance with a county constituency. And perhaps a chimpanzee would be a cleverer animal than this Ghosh Baboo, whose publicly uttered sentiments in Dacca obtained for him the distinguishing title of polecat. Thank Heaven! four hundred do not represent an English constituency, and the Baboo may find to his cost that at the last moment the English nationality has revived. In such a case his insolence and presumption in seeking a seat in Parliament would be fitly rewarded by an infuriate crowd of roughs!"

The accomplished Indian gentleman to whom the above remarks refer was President of the Indian National Congress held at Madras in 1903.

great mass of the working-classes in England to a policy of friendliness to Indian aspirations and support of the Indian national movement. There is progress in the press, which every day devotes more attention to India. Of all newspapers the *Times* is the greatest power in this direction. With its immense influence and general attitude of avowed hostility to the Indian movement, it is honourably distinguished by the liberality and hospitality it affords to the expression of views diametrically opposed to its own. The increasing strength of public opinion in England is undoubted. There is greater moderation, and the growth of opinion advances on irresistible lines in increasing sympathy with the Indian people, and an increased sense of England's responsibility for India's welfare. Every year there is an addition to the number of those who avow doctrines which were formerly condemned as unpatriotic and unreasonable, and who, in their appeal to a higher tribunal than national self-love, are gradually leavening the tone of public opinion by their persistent enthusiasm, and profoundly modifying existing conceptions.

Some of the best books about India have been written by men who have had no official concern with the country, who have perhaps never even visited it, and who derive all their knowledge of it from indirect sources. Such books will often contain more valuable reflections on the nature of our administration of India, on the constitution of our Empire, on the effects of our rule, and on the dangers (external and internal) which may befall it, and they offer also more valuable suggestions in regard to the future of India, than are usually to be found in similar books put forth by Indian officials of the widest experience. There is an advantage in being untrammelled by official antecedents. The opinions of those who have passed long years of service in India are unconsciously weighed down and narrowed by a bias derived from their whole life and environment. Many admirable books about India have, indeed, been written by Anglo-Indians, officials and non-officials; but the tendency of officials is to exalt unduly the excellence of the work on which they have been themselves engaged, and err on the side of excessive self-laudation.

It results from this unfortunate but natural tendency, that it is necessary to make a wide allowance for the optimistic character of most Anglo-Indian writers; and the higher the official rank of the authority, the more sure is he to be an apologist, or perhaps biographer, of his own administration, and the more needful it is to discount his conclusions. The disinterested labours of such men as Evans-Bell, Osborn, and Geddes, who died before they could accomplish their work, and of many living officers who, in their retirement, devote their unflagging energies to the true interests of India, are notable exceptions to this general rule. But the fact remains that it is not in the volumes annually published by Anglo-Indian administrators that we may look for any glimmer of insight into that utter derangement of economic and social conditions which our conquest has wrought, and which is the chief cause of the pauperisation of the people. Nor is it likely that in these volumes we shall find any perception of the deteriorating effect wrought upon both conquerors and conquered by the anomalous relations existing between them. These are elements of cardinal importance in considering whether, on the whole, our presence in India has been for good or for evil; and yet their very existence is commonly ignored in the writings of official apologists. The pessimist writers who have the courage and ability to express their opinions discharge, therefore, a useful function, which will continue to be necessary so long as officials like Sir Henry Fowler and Sir John Strachey continue to maintain that our Indian Government is the most beneficent, most perfect, and most unalterable that can be imagined. Unfortunately their work is for the most part critical only ; it may wither and destroy, but it does not replace. The real need of India is reconstruction ; and it is the special value of such utterances as those of Osborn, Caird, Blunt, and Congreve that they lead directly to the formation of administrative principles on which a reconstructive policy can be based.

I would mention the name of the late Mr William Digby with respect, though I cannot agree with all his conclusions. Mr Digby rendered a valuable service by drawing the attention of the British public to India's poverty. Sir James Caird's book is full of useful and practical suggestions. The letters of Mr Wilfred Scawen Blunt, which were written many years ago, and were republished under the title of *Ideas about India*, are conspicuous illustrations of keen insight into the real relations between England and India. The outburst of indignation they excited among Anglo-Indians is an nstructive contrast to the impression they created among the Indian community, which was briefly one of mingled surprise and gratification that an Englishman who had only travelled in India for a few months should be able so thoroughly to understand and represent their feelings. More recently the deliberate utterances of Mr William Jennings Bryan and Mr Andrew Carnegie, so full of penetration into Indian problems and of sympathy with the Indian people, are a remarkable evidence of American interest in India which must powerfully react on English opinion. The publication during the past year of a volume entitled *L'Inde contemporaine et le mouvement national*, by M. Ernest Piriou,—a brilliant, accurate, and lucid exposition of Indian opinion and aspirations,—is an encouraging indication of sympathetic interest from the Continent of Europe. Our obligations are due to the late Sir William Hunter, whose unquenchable optimism impairs but does not destroy the value of his vivid interpretations of India to the English reader. Mr Romesh Dutt, with great erudition and exemplary industry, has devoted himself to the elucidation of elaborate studies on the economic and historic aspects of Indian life. Mr Dadabhai Naoroji, Sir William Wedderburn, Henry Fawcett, Charles Bradlaugh, and the late Mr Caine, whose premature death all India still mourns, have devoted their great influence, both in and out of Parliament, to the interests of India in this country. I may cite greater names who have wrought still more in the formation of public opinion in England on India. Edmund Burke will always be preeminent for his profound sympathy with the people of India, and for the extraordinary knowledge of the country he acquired. The eloquence of his utterances has made them household words among us, and ensures their influence for all time. The writings and speeches of Macaulay have rendered inestimable service by popularising and establishing on a broad basis the application of liberal principles in practical administration and policy. The noblest and most eloquent of modern statesmen also, Mr Gladstone and Mr Bright, have stirred the heart of Englishmen, and deservedly earned the gratitude of the people of India by recalling England to a sense of her duties to her great dependency.

The essential importance of English opinion in regard to India will be best appreciated if we measure what the effect of such opinion has been in regard to Irish reform. Internal agitation in Ireland has always been useless; it was only when Irish agitation was supplemented by a powerful phalanx of opinion in England that any concessions were allowed to the sister island. And so it is in the case of India. There is, I am persuaded, no reason to justify the fears of those who look on the peaceful solution of the Indian problem as a mere speculative contingency, altogether outside the sphere of practical politics. But we know that internal pressure is powerless; it leads to repression only, the ultimate outcome of which must be a national outbreak. The experiment of a "firm and resolute government" in Ireland has been tried in vain, and the adoption of a similar policy in India is inevitably destined to fail. The remedy for both countries is the same. The opportunity of a peaceful solution rests in both cases with the English people, who alone have it in their hands to effect a material modification in the attitude of Government through the pressure of public opinion from the mother country.

The powerlessness of any action which may originate in India itself is illustrated by the history of Lord Ripon's administration. It is impossible that I can mention Lord Ripon's name in terms of too high praise. From the moment he landed in India to the day he left it he laboured for the native population. His tenure of office will always be a memorable one.

He will be known in history as the author of a progressive and enlightened policy, as a statesman of wide and sincere sympathy with the people of the country, above all others "the Friend of India"; and it will be the proudest honour of his successors if their names are handed down to posterity with that of Ripon. Yet he was able to accomplish little. It is true that the political revolution now taking place in India is largely attributable to his exertions—although, by the irony of fate, it is far more largely attributable to the blind fanaticism of those who opposed him—but the actual results of his administration as shown upon the statute-book are not very great. I recognise the difficulties by which he was surrounded, and it may be that he was encompassed by other difficulties of which I have no knowledge. He was harassed and hampered in an inconceivable degree by the bigotry and race feeling of his own fellow-countrymen. He was paralysed from want of support, and neither he nor any man in his position single-handed could have overcome the dead wall of opposition by which he was confronted.

I take this opportunity (before I allude further to Lord Ripon's policy) of linking the present with the past, and of invoking for his predecessors and successors their due tribute of acknowledgment. I do this advisedly, for I am able to bear testimony to the good which has been done; and I think there is too great a tendency among those who are impressed with the injustice of the English conquest to look with jaundiced eyes on all features of Indian administration. We may condemn the conquest (as animated by unworthy motives, for which no adequate justification has ever been brought forward), but we need not blind ourselves to the advantages which have followed from it. If it has been the case that, almost without exception, every Governor-General has extended the area of British territory, it is also the case that every Governor-General has taken his part in consolidating a peaceful administration over the territory so acquired. If the external policy of Government has been one of systematic aggression, it is also true that the internal policy has been one of continual progress. To Warren Hastings we are indebted for the endowment of Oriental learning on an assured basis. To Lord Cornwallis we owe the foundation of the present form of the civil administration, the purification of the Civil Service, and the priceless boon of a permanent land settlement in Bengal. To Lord William Bentinck we owe the establishment of the principle that no natives of India are to be excluded by reason of their birth from any appointments under Government.[1] To Lord Metcalfe we owe the freedom of the press. We owe to Lord William Bentinck, under the inspiration of Macaulay, the foundation of an educational system which has revolutionised India. The establishment of Medical Colleges is due to Lord William Bentinck and to Lord Auckland. It is to Lord Hardinge that we owe the public and solemn announcement of an assurance that "in every possible case a preference shall be given, in the selection of candidates for public employment, to those who have been educated in the Institutions established

[1] As long ago as 1833 it was provided by Act of Parliament "that no native of the said territories, nor any natural-born subject of Her Majesty resident therein, shall, by reason only of his religion, place of birth, descent, colour, or any of them, be disabled from holding any place, office, or employment under the said Company." The same assurance was conveyed by the Queen's proclamation of 1858, when the Government of India was transferred from the Company to the Crown. And so it was observed by Lord Northbrook in the House of Lords, "Whether it was Lord Dalhousie, with his imperial instincts, or Lord Canning, with the responsibility laid upon him of dealing with the Mutiny, or Lord Lawrence, with his great knowledge of the internal organisation of the country, or Lord Mayo, associated from childhood with the Conservative party—all alike held that there should be no distinction of class or race, and that there should be one law for all classes of Her Majesty's subjects."

for the instruction of the people, as well by the Government as by private individuals and societies." To Lord Dalhousie we owe the initiation of a policy for developing the resources of the country which is now bearing fruit. His name is also associated with the establishment of Universities in India. The memory of Lord Canning will always be cherished by the Indian people for his justice, his firmness and courage at the time of a great crisis, and for his clemency. To Sir John Lawrence we owe the municipalisation of the large towns;[1] to Lord Mayo the decentralisation of the finances. To the humanity of Lord Northbrook we are indebted for the definite and practical assertion of the principle that it is the first duty of the Administration during famine to preserve life. To

[1] The following utterance of Sir John Lawrence, on 31st August 1864, distinctly foreshadows our present policy:—"Great public benefit is to be expected from the firm establishment of a system of municipal administration in India. Neither the central Government nor the local governments are capable of providing either the funds or the executive agency for making the improvements of various kinds in all the cities and towns of India which are demanded by the rapidly developing wealth of the country. The people of India are quite capable of administering their own affairs; the municipal feeling is deeply rooted in them. The village communities, each of which is a little republic, are the most abiding of Indian institutions. Holding the position we do in India, every view of duty and policy should induce us to leave as much as possible of the business of the country to be done by the people."

Lords Dufferin and Lansdowne we owe the establishment of Legislative Councils upon a more or less popular basis. There are few indeed of the Governor-Generals of India whose names we may not associate with large and enlightened measures for the welfare, education, or political training of the people.

I venture, therefore, to think that the progress already made is a fit subject for commemoration. It is well to remember that a policy of consolidation has proceeded hand in hand with a career of conquest, that the establishment of order is always essential to any real progress, and that the united and continuous efforts of previous generations are the necessary introduction to all great measures of reform. If the war epoch has at last drawn to a close, if the conquest of India is complete, and our future proconsuls may sigh with Alexander that they have no more worlds to conquer, if all the energies of the Indian Government may now be devoted to the encouragement of national reconstruction—the vantage position we thus occupy is entirely due to the labours of our predecessors. It is they who have prepared the way for the pending changes which are about to affect every portion of the Empire. It is well to acknowledge that great progress has been already made in imparting civilisation, education, and order, and that the mechanism of one of the most remarkable movements ever known in the world has been set going by the hand of Government.

The policy of Lord Ripon was thus described by an acute but hostile critic in the House of Lords: "It is the policy of gradually transferring political power in India from European to native hands." "Does it not mean," asked Lord Lytton,[1] "nay, ought it not to be taken as meaning that we, the English Government in India, feel ourselves in a false position, from which we wish to extricate ourselves as quickly as possible? We must, no doubt, hold office for a certain time, in order to train up you natives to take our places; but this is our only object. As soon as it is accomplished (and the sooner the better), we shall retire, and leave India to be governed by whatever body her native representative assemblies may see fit to entrust with the task of government." This is Lord Lytton's language, not mine; it is a paraphrase uttered by a politician who had himself been Viceroy, with a full sense of responsibility and knowledge that his words were not likely to be forgotten.

It is true that Lord Ripon himself was careful to abstain from any such outspoken avowal, and

[1] As reported in the *Times*, 10th April 1883.

that his friends and supporters were but too ready to offer the excuse that the proposals which excited so much bitter and violent opposition were really isolated in character and individually of small importance. It is true that the language of Lord Lytton was at once deprecated by Her Majesty's Ministers in that half-hearted manner in which the Liberal Government is too apt to protest against conclusions which must ensue from the conscientious application of its professed principles. It would therefore be incorrect to say that either the Liberal Ministry at home or Lord Ripon in India had consciously identified themselves with the policy which Lord Lytton enunciated on their behalf. On the contrary, it is probable that Lord Ripon was, in the first instance, as unconscious of the inevitable tendency of his own measures as he was admittedly unprepared for the tremendous opposition their introduction provoked. At the same time it would be unjust to deny to Lord Ripon the most ample credit for a great work. He was the instrument at whose hands a long and elaborate preparation at last received its due fulfilment. But he was a great deal more than a mere instrument. The policy which he espoused is indeed the logical development of principles which all previous Viceroys—even

Lord Lytton himself—had been ripening to maturity. But it was Lord Ripon who took action far more decided than any of his predecessors, who by his own personal enthusiasm infused life into the dry bones of the dull office machine, and by the vigour of his example stimulated the subordinate governments to give practical expression to his views. Already the benevolent despotism of an autocratic administration is merging into a system of free representation and municipal and local independence. The way is being gradually prepared for the emancipation of the Indian people. There has been no change in the power of Government, which is still as supreme as that of the Czar of Russia. The Government of India is still characterised by its absolutely despotic constitution. But it is in the spirit and disposition with which supreme power is exercised that a change is visible. We have seen the complete reversal of an aggressive policy on the North-West Frontier. After having been for nearly fifty years under British rule, the province of Mysore was lately restored to its hereditary prince, and for the first time in the history of India the red line of British possessions has receded. The Guicowar of Baroda was restored to his dominions. In spite of unprecedented provocation, the little State of Manipore was not annexed. A system of provincial representation has been introduced into the local legislatures. A comprehensive scheme of local self-government has been organised. An Indian judge has been appointed more than once to officiate as Chief Justice of the High Court. It is frankly acknowledged that Indian politics have entered upon a new phase, and that the demand of educated Indians for a share in the government of their country is one of the most important factors of the new problem which we have to face. The power and influence of public opinion is recognised, and the voice of the people can be no longer ignored.

The period of Lord Ripon and of his Finance Minister, who is now Lord Cromer, has been well described as the Golden Age of Indian reformers, when the aspirations of the people were encouraged, education and local self-government were fostered, and the foundations of Indian nationality were firmly laid. The natural trend of Anglo-Indian opinion has been to assert itself in a reactionary outburst against this development, disparaging the vantage-ground acquired in the past. In the Imperialism of Lord Curzon these reactionary tendencies were afforded a too willing mouthpiece. We have been told that the salvation of India is not to be sought on the field of politics at the present stage of her development; that there are many other fields of usefulness and power which lie around the citadel of politics, and that when these fields are occupied the entrance to real political life will be easy, natural, and safe. We must, it is said, "wearily retrace our steps and devote our energies to educating the Indians in character and common-sense. Then, and not till then, can we put them out into the polytechnic of local self-government." We must wait for a working reality "until generations and generations of really educated Indians have come and gone." We have been told that the weakness and limitations of the newly educated classes are now more clearly perceived, and that the complexities of the problems of Oriental politics are more distinctly realised. We are familiar with these considerations, for they are the commonplaces of reaction.

But it is not by indulgence in such vague generalities that the current of advance can be stemmed. Of what avail is it to disparage Burke and Macaulay and Bright, Ripon, Cromer, and Elphinstone? You cannot withstand the flowing tide. Temporary spasms of reaction are inevitable. They pass away like footprints on the sand, and we need not trouble ourselves too much with these vexatious aberrations from the path of progress. They will be quickly forgotten.

In the meantime the reactionary principles of administration, although they are discredited, cannot be formally destroyed until they are replaced ; and for the Government to accomplish this is no easy task. It is not every Viceroy in India who is able to resist the pressure brought to bear on him by his own countrymen. It requires the assurance of a strong moral support from home,—support not from the English Government only, but from the English people.

It is a common complaint that the politics of India find no echo in the life and interests of Englishmen. Nothing short of a great famine or a great Durbar, a great earthquake or a terrible pestilence, a victory or a defeat, will attract attention to our vast dependency. It is perhaps inevitable that this should be so. But the spirit of indifferentism is hardly less dangerous than the spirit of the new Imperialism. England is a great nation, with vast responsibilities, unique and unparalleled in their wide-reaching influence and operation. England's Empire is India, before which even our great Colonies pale into comparative insignificance. It is with Englishmen that the great questions on which the fate of India depends must ultimately be decided. It is our privilege, the privilege of our people, to assist and determine action and to formulate policy.

It is often asked whether it is desirable to make Indian questions party questions, or to deal with them on non-party lines. The answer lies in a nutshell. We want more attention to be attracted to Indian affairs in England. Why is it that such apathy prevails? It is because India is outside the arena of party conflict. How often is India referred to by any candidate for Parliament in his election address? "We are all agreed that it is best and wisest to exclude India from the field of our ordinary party operations." Those are the words of Mr Morley.[1] They are true if we are to regard "our ordinary party politics" as an ignoble struggle for office. But they are not true if they mean that the principles of Liberalism are not as applicable to Indian as to English affairs. Under a Tory Government we find a policy of race and class domination, of disregard of the people's wishes, of aggression abroad and repression at home. Under a Liberal Government we expect to see

[1] In his speech on the Indian Budget, 20th July 1906.

a negation of this policy. We want more members for India. We want to hear more of India in the House of Commons. We want more members of the House who will devote themselves to India as an integral and vital part of the British dominions, as a portion of the Empire which is not directly represented, and calls therefore for special attention. But where and how are we to find such representation? In former times we heard nothing of this cry that India must be shut out of party politics. Many of the most memorable debates in the House of Commons in which Burke and Dundas, Pitt and Fox, and, later on, Macaulay took part, were Indian discussions conducted on party lines. Those who urge that India should not be made a party question are always those who do not wish Indian questions to be discussed in England. The hope of India lies, however, in such discussion, and the realisation of that hope will only be fulfilled when there arises another Burke or Bright who shall restore the lost tradition, and, by the force of his eloquence and influence, raise Indian politics to the level of colonial or foreign or domestic politics upon which party government hangs together, and on which the fate of a Liberal or Conservative Administration depends.

I do not deny that English opinion may be profitably exercised on particular subjects, but it is of greater importance that it should be directed to moulding general principles. I remember the words of Mr Gladstone when he spoke in the House of Commons[1] of the relations between Parliament and the Indian Government. He said: "It is not our business to advise what machinery the Indian Government should use. It is our business to give to those representing Her Majesty's Government in India ample information as to what we believe to be sound principles of government. It is also the duty and function of this House to comment upon any case in which we think the authorities in India have failed to give due effect to those principles; but in the discharge of their high administrative functions, or as to the choice of means, there is no doubt that that should be left in their hands." These words were wise. They do not imply any abnegation of the responsibilities of Parliament for the good government of India, and there is little echo in them of the pitiful appeal of the official bureaucracy to preserve India from Parliamentary interference. But they are a timely reminder that it is not by attempting to rule directly a

[1] Debate on the Indian Councils Bill, June 1892.

country like India that we can do our duty to that distant territory. The details of administration must be left in the hands of those who possess a competent knowledge of Indian affairs, upon whom must always rest the personal responsibility of giving effect to a reconstructive policy without disturbance. For them there is good and noble work remaining to be done. The difficulties accompanying the present epoch of excitement can only be successfully overcome by the cordial co-operation of local officials during the crisis. By the exercise of personal influence, which, in virtue of their position, is almost indescribably great, by the force of a strong example of tolerance, courtesy, and good-will, they have it in their power to do much to temper prestige and pride, and to establish a more kindly relationship with the people. For us, our duties lie in a different direction. Busied with the ordinary affairs of life, it is not possible for us to familiarise ourselves with the details of Indian administration. Our interests are nearer home. But our responsibilities remain. The white man's burden is on us. Our duty is to make ourselves acquainted far more nearly than we do at present with the current events and history of India—so much, indeed, is easy—but, above all, on the basis of such acquaintance to form convictions on the general policy which should guide the Government, and to labour in the creation of a popular opinion which shall share those convictions, and stimulate and strengthen the authorities in putting them into practice.

Those, at least, who think as I do need not hesitate to offer such aid as they can give. We have no cause for hesitation. We are already armed for the encounter, and have no difficulty in formulating the principles which we think should be followed. We accept the fundamental doctrine of modern social life, the subordination of politics to morals. We claim to test our political action by moral considerations, allowing that for the State as well as for individuals it is the question not of rights but of duties that must take precedence. These are the new principles we have to offer in substitution of the worn-out ideas which have provisionally been employed. This is our policy of reconstruction. The policy of the future—which is based alike on the duty of England and on the need of India, on the devotion which is due from a strong nation to a weak and subject people—must be a policy of national self-sacrifice, voluntary restitution, and disinterested moderation.

POLITICAL RECONSTRUCTION

THERE are, I suppose, not many reflecting persons who will maintain that our occupation of India, as we hold it, can be of a permanent character. The emancipation of India has become inevitable ever since a system of English education was established and the principle of political equality accepted. The great upheaval which has revolutionised all departments of Indian thought, inspired the aspirations of diverse communities, and infused the sense of nationality throughout a vast and surging empire, can only find its peaceful fulfilment in the wise and prescient recognition of changes imminent in the situation which the British Government itself has created. The Right Honourable Mountstuart Elphinstone wrote, as long ago as 1850:—

I conceive that the administration of all the departments of a great country by a small number of foreign visitors, in a state of isolation produced by a difference in religion, ideas, and manners, which cuts them off from all intimate communion with the people, can never be contemplated as a permanent state of things. I conceive also that the progress of education among the natives renders such a scheme impracticable, even if it were otherwise free from objection. It might, perhaps, have once been possible to have retained the natives in a subordinate condition (at the expense of national justice and honour) by studiously repressing their spirit and discouraging their progress in knowledge; but we are now doing our best to raise them in all mental qualities to a level with ourselves, and to instil into them the liberal opinions in government and policy which have long prevailed in this country, and it is vain to endeavour to rule them on principles only suited to a slavish and ignorant population.

These words are a lasting tribute to the sagacity of the old Anglo-Indian statesman who had lived for thirty years in India, who had ruled as Governor of Bombay for eight years, to whom the Governor-Generalship of India was twice offered, and who in honoured retirement in the evening of his life had lost none of his sympathetic interest in the country he had served so well. The experience of more than half a century since they were written merely confirms their truth.

I will supplement them by a quotation from

one who is universally recognised as the greatest and most successful of Britain's proconsuls. More than twenty years have now elapsed since Lord Cromer said :—

No one who watches the signs of the times in India with even moderate care can doubt that we have entered upon a period of change. The spread of education, the increasing influence of a free press, the substitution of legal for discretionary administration, the progress of railways and telegraphs, the easier communication with Europe, and the more ready influx of European ideas, are beginning to produce a marked effect upon the people. New ideas are springing up. New aspirations are being called forth. The power of public opinion is growing daily. Such a condition of affairs is one in which the task of Government, and especially of a despotic Government, is beset with difficulties of no light kind. To move too fast is dangerous, but to lag behind is more dangerous still. The problem is how to deal with this new-born spirit of progress, raw and superficial as in many respects it is, so as to direct it into the right course, and to derive from it all the benefits which its development is capable of ultimately conferring upon the country, and at the same time to prevent it from becoming, through blind indifference or stupid repression, a source of serious political danger. It is only what ought to be expected by every thoughtful man, that, after fifty years of free press and thirty years of expanding education, with European ideas flowing into the country on every side, and old indigenous customs, habits, and prejudices breaking down, changes should be taking place in the thoughts, the desires, and the aims of the intelligent and educated men of the country which no wise and cautious Government can afford to disregard, and to which they must gradually adapt their system of administration if they do not wish to see it shattered by forces which they have themselves called into being, but which they have failed to guide and control.

This quotation is a long one, but it is fraught with wisdom, and it is needless to say that during the twenty years which have since elapsed the conditions mentioned by Lord Cromer have developed with increasing rapidity.

We have to deal with a problem of much difficulty and complexity. India is a tutelage unexampled in history, and we have incurred liabilities on its account not lightly to be set aside. Lord Curzon once declared that he could not conceive of a time as remotely possible when it would be either practicable or desirable that Great Britain should take her hand from the Indian plough. Bnt such is not my conception of India's future. It is vain, and worse than vain, it is the purest folly, fraught with danger to ourselves, "to continue to rule on worn-out lines which are only suited to a slavish and ignorant population." A wise and cautious

Government must gradually adapt its system of administration to the changing grooves of political reconstruction on new principles, which, however they may be delayed or marred in the execution, are sure in the event. The character of the work which lies before us is difficult and delicate. England should no more break from its past than should India break from the traditions of its history. An abrupt retreat would, as has been well said, be to act like a man who should kidnap a child, and then, in a fit of repentance, abandon him in a tiger jungle. The process of reconstruction can be effected only by slow and gradual means. Many years must elapse, generations may pass away, before we can expect the consummation of the policy I advocate. But it is a policy which we should always keep before our eyes, and to which all our efforts should converge. Sooner or later India must again take her own rank among the nations of the East, and our action should be devoted to facilitating her progress to freedom. Not in mere vague talk, but strenuously and of set purpose, it should be the principal object of our Indian Government to address itself to the peaceful reconstruction of native administrations in its own place.

The task is not so stupendous as at first

appears. The difficulty is not so much to organise internal administration as to provide for the existence of healthy relations between separate and independent States. But even in this respect the difficulties are exaggerated. It would ill become Englishmen who are actually engaged in a daily policy of dangerous repression to confess themselves incapable of political reconstruction.

The best solution of the problem is apparently to be found in the proposal to place India on a fraternal footing with the Colonies of England. A constitutional relationship of this kind, as though England were the parent country and India its colony, would form a material guarantee for the peaceful attitude of the federated States. England will always have a stake in India sufficient to call forth interference if necessary; and in the event of a civil war in India, the military interposition of England would be required in the interest of both countries. England herself, therefore, will continue to afford the principal guarantee of peace.

Autonomy, and not assimilation, is the keynote of England's true relations with her great Colonies. It is the keynote also of India's destiny. It is more than this: it is the destiny of the world. The tendency of empire in the civilised world is in the direction of compact autonomous States, which are federated together and attached by common motives to a central power. In the United States of America, with their vast and compact area and fairly homogeneous population, autonomy and assimilation have been happily combined. In the Old World, Continental States have settled themselves within narrower limits, and are less troubled than Great Britain with the complex problems of extended Empire. But, generally speaking, they are compact powers linked together by common memories and associations and common objects. Local autonomy has been conceded where the difficulties of assimilation would otherwise have been insuperable in the face of local interests or of an irreconcilable national spirit. None are in a better position than Englishmen to appreciate the value of this principle in fostering national progress and material wealth. In our Canadian Dominion and in Australasia autonomy has long ago been granted to its full extent, and we have established a Federal Government in a Commonwealth of autonomous States. These Colonies have all the elements of great and growing nations. We have enjoyed in the amplest measure the reward of this policy in that union of hearts between

Colonists and Englishmen which forms a far firmer guarantee of national prosperity than could ever be found in any scheme for representation in an Imperial Council, or in incorporation into one military and commercial Empire. It is due to the sagacious prescience of our great Liberal Statesmen during a past generation that the Colonies were given that varied and supple constitution and practical independence which are the basis and condition of their friendly concert in the Imperial policy of the parent State. We are now according responsible government on similar lines to South Africa. Freedom, so far from weakening the bonds between England and her Colonies, has cemented them ; and we have only to look to the outburst of loyalty and affection, of which we reaped the harvest during the South African war, to know that our Liberal Statesmen were wise and right.

It is in accordance with these precedents that I foresee the ultimate solution of political reconstruction in India. The circumstances of Russia afford us no parallel. In itself historically and geographically more of an Oriental than a Western power, Russia has without much effort or deliberate policy absorbed the border tribes on its eastern frontier, and all its extensions eastward have been conterminous with its own natural and ever-widening boundaries. In this way it has by a sure and almost unconscious process assimilated vast areas of Northern and Central Asia up to the confines of the Pacific. Assimilation has been complete, but there is no autonomy, for Russia has none to give. The relations of England with India are in striking contrast to those of Russia with Central Asia. We have not simply overstepped our borders, and our contact with the East is not the incorporation of neighbouring States.

There can be no assimilation between Englishmen and the natives of India, separated from us by many thousand miles of land and sea. But, in accordance with an august and liberal policy, we have extended to India the inestimable boons of education, political equality, and representation. The dawn of the day has risen which Macaulay declared in the House of Commons would be the proudest day in England's history. His eloquent and prophetic utterance ought always to be ringing in our ears :—

> The destinies of our Indian Empire are covered with thick darkness. It is difficult to form any conjecture as to the fate reserved for a State which resembles no other in history and which forms by itself a separate class of political phenomena. The laws which regulate its growth and its decay are still

unknown to us. It may be that the public mind of India may expand under our system till it has outgrown our system; that by good government we may educate our subjects into a capacity for better government; that having become instructed in European knowledge, they may in some future age demand European institutions. Whether such a day will ever come I know not. But never will I attempt to avert or retard it. Whenever it comes, it will be the proudest day in England's history. To have found a great people sunk in the lowest depths of slavery and superstition, to have so ruled them as to have made them desirous and capable of all the privileges of citizens, would indeed be a title to glory all our own. The sceptre may pass away from us. Unforeseen accidents may derange our most profound schemes of policy. Victory may be inconstant to our arms. But there are triumphs which are followed by no reverse. There is an empire exempt from all natural causes of decay. Those triumphs are the pacific triumphs of reason over barbarism; that empire is the imperishable empire of our arts and our morals, our literature and our laws.

The full development of autonomy is still in a distant future, but the beginnings have been laid and the paths have been made straight. The claim for representation in the Government of Great Britain is frequently put forward in the advanced organs of Indian thought, and Indian candidates have often stood for Parliament.

This need not excite our wonder when we consider how the glamour of a Parliamentary career dazzles men's eyes. But it would be more fitting and I am sure more gratifying to the ambition and energies of these able and cultivated Indians if they were afforded a larger and more appropriate outlet in the administration of their own country. A certain measure of representation has already been accorded to the Indian people in the local legislatures. It is in its further development, in the increase of their power and influence in India itself, and not in representation in England, that we shall find the appropriate and natural prize and legitimate goal for Indian aspirations.

In the face of the bloated armaments of Europe, it may seem useless to speculate about the reduction of the English army in India. But with a proper reorganisation of the native army it should be possible to effect a material diminution in the number of English troops required. There are only two ways of governing a conquered country ; there is no safe standing-point between absolute suppression and absolute equality. The last is the goal to which we tend, and in military no less than civil reconstruction it is necessary to identify the interest of individuals with the State. The native army is, however, now organised on a mercenary basis. It is more and more replenished by rude and ignorant recruits from the borders of our frontier or beyond it, and the martial spirit of our own Indian subjects is gradually dying out. "Tribes," writes Sir Richard Temple, "which fifty years ago were notoriously attached to arms, are now comparatively unwarlike. With training and discipline the troops will still behave very well; but with the masses of them there is hardly now the predilection for the fight, the instinct of physical contention, that there used to be." The Mogul emperors adopted heartily and completely the policy of trust; Akbar's greatest generals and most devoted adherents were children of the very men his grandfather had conquered; the Rajput chivalry was the main bulwark of the Mogul throne. The British Government, on the contrary, has adopted a policy of suspicion; the Indian officers of our native army are only old soldiers, promoted from the ranks, who in virtue of their longer services draw larger pay, and are permitted to sit down in the presence of an English subaltern. We can expect no assistance from such men, and we get none. The Russians can get from the territories they have absorbed in Central Asia an Alikhanoff or a Loris Melikoff. We can only produce men who rise to the rank of Naik, Havildar, or Resaldar, or to some other subordinate post, the name of which perplexes the English public. The first step towards the reorganisation of the native army is to augment the power of the native officers, to afford some scope to their abilities and ambition, and to raise them to a level with ourselves. Lord Curzon has already moved in this direction. His commendable object was to attract into our armies the gentlemen and aristocracy of the country. I am told that his attempt has not proved very successful. It was launched on a very small scale. But if pursued with due encouragement and persistence, it will afford a powerful impetus towards the conversion of the native mercenary army into a national force. A further step is required. The decentralisation (if it may so be called) of the native army is the logical complement of Lord Curzon's policy. The establishment of provincial army corps, with an *esprit* and traditions of their own, recruited from the common people, and officered by the native gentry of the provinces in which they are to serve, would prove both a safeguard against internal disorder and a protection against attack from without. Just as the Rajputs and Mussulmans under the Moguls formed separate armies with their national chiefs, and, inspired by rivalry, distinguished themselves by feats of valour which are still remembered, so the provincial armies of the future, animated by a similar emulation, would display equal valour and hardihood in fighting for a common cause.

The native remedy—the permission to volunteer—is another proposal which tends in the same direction of the gradual disbandment of mercenaries and English soldiers. The agitation in favour of volunteering has been set on foot, and is sustained entirely by educated natives of the country. It is primarily the outcome of an honourable feeling that as they ask for a larger share in the administration, and to be allowed to exercise the privileges and rights of citizens, so they ought not to shrink from their national duties. But this feeling is also allied with others equally honourable. As the late Sir Henry Harrison, in the pamphlet I have already quoted, well says :[1]—

> The desire to be enrolled as volunteers arises (1) from a wish for political equality, a desire not to be regarded as Helots while other sections of the community are regarded as Spartans ; (2) from a conviction that those who claim their share in the prizes of administration must show their willingness to bear their share of the burdens of the citizenship ; (3) from

[1] *Ought Natives to be welcomed as Volunteers?* p. 22.

a knowledge that the Bengalees and other Indian races are physically degenerate, and a desire to do something, however little, to make them less effeminate; (4) from a pride in association with a noble Empire like that over which Her Majesty presides, and a desire to share in its glories by being numbered among its defenders; (5) from a conviction that a struggle may be imminent in India between the forces of retrogression led by Russia and those of progress led by England, and that their sympathies and their fortunes must unhesitatingly and unwaveringly be thrown in with the latter.

The enthusiasm which the educated natives evinced on this subject was very remarkable, and it was echoed by the Indian press with singular earnestness and unanimity. The Government repressed it with a cold refusal; but if persistence will bear any proportion to the determination expressed, it is a movement calculated to exercise a considerable influence in modifying the future constitution of our armies, and in keeping alive the military spirit of the country.

In civil administration the need of a similar policy is more evident and has made more way. The tendency towards decentralisation, though momentarily discouraged, is firmly established, and is eventually destined to resolve itself into a federated union such as prevails in the Federation of Australia and in the Canadian Dominion. Provincial representative government will gradually lead to the development and definition of the peculiar idiosyncrasy of each federated State. It is a noble and exalted duty that is reserved to our fellow-countrymen who are responsible for the destinies of India. It is theirs to guide and facilitate the transition. The ideal of political reconstruction is a federation of States under the supremacy of England, with provincial national armies gradually replacing the standing army of Great Britain. The careful conservation of existing social institutions is the essential supplement of this reconstruction. The country recoils from such a social revolution as our Western civilisation has thrust upon it. It still needs the hierarchical leadership of caste. The tendency to reduce the power of the dominant classes, and to destroy, if possible, all distinction between the different strata of society, is much in vogue among headstrong administrators, who are too apt to transplant the radical associations of our democracy into a country altogether unsuited to their growth. But there is no more patrician *milieu* in the world than that which has for centuries flourished in India, and still is vigorous, in spite of attacks upon it. Lord Lytton, at the time of the "Kaisar-i-Hind Durbar" at Delhi, appointed a few of the principal chiefs in India to be Councillors of the Empire, but the sound instinct which marked his action has not been revived, and these "pillars of state" have never been invited to take their part in Imperial deliberations. Lord Curzon, who is endowed with no small measure of Oriental insight, might have been expected to appreciate the value of this association of the Government with the aristocracy of the Empire. But he showed no sign. It is not, however, too late to attract to the nation's councils the great noblemen of India. "I sometimes think," said Mr Morley in his Budget speech,[1] "that we make a mistake in not attaching the weight we should to these powerful princes as standing forces in India." There is hope, therefore, that the question may be again raised. It would be a great step in political reconstruction.

The sympathetic and systematic encouragement of the government of the feudatory States is another natural link in the same direction. Some of these States—such as Mysore, Travancore, and Baroda—have shown that, in the hands of their enlightened chiefs, models of administration may be looked for under indigenous rule. Opportunity in their case has brought efficiency

[1] On the 20th July 1906.

along with it. The names of Sir Dinkar Rao, Sir Madhava Rao, and Sir Salar Jung—not to mention other ministers of equal ability, although perhaps of less fame—are sufficient evidence of the aptitude and skill with which the affairs of large and important independent territories have been administered. What is required, in the absence of an emasculating foreign army, is an organisation of small States, each with a prince at its head, and a small body of patrician aristocracy interposing between him and the lower orders of working-men. For such an arrangement the country appears to be eminently adapted; the United States of India should be bound together by means of some political organisation other than the colonial supremacy of England. The basis of internal order is to be found in the recognition of a patriciate accustomed by hereditary associations to control and lead.

Even the Mahomedan community is largely influenced by caste practices derived from its long contact with the Hindoo system. The Mahomedans as well as the Hindoos are thus well fitted for an aristocratic form of government. The difference between the Hindoo and Mahomedan religions would not at all stand in the way of the establishment of a similar form of government in both cases. The difference in religion is, however, one of the greatest practical difficulties in any scheme of reconstruction. I do not forget that the principal officers of State under the great Akbar were Hindoos; that the chief officers under Hyder Ali were also Hindoos; and that the ablest prime minister of Runjeet Singh, the man who kept his policy straight, was a Mahomedan. The Mogul dynasty was generally dependent on Hindoo agency in all matters of administrative detail. These instances give ground for hope that a principle of social unity between the chiefs and aristocracies of the Hindoo and Mahomedan classes may some day be established. At the same time it is impossible to be blind to the general character of the relations between Hindoos and Mahomedans; to the jealousy which exists and manifests itself so frequently, even under British rule, in local outbursts of popular fanaticism; to the kine-killing riots and to the religious friction which occasionally accompanies the celebration of the Ram Lila or the Bakir Eed or the Mohurrum. These are practical difficulties which the Government must always be prepared to face. Where there are unsympathising, not to say hostile, relations, the obstacles in the way of assimilation are unquestionably very great. Time and the impulse of educational influences can alone afford the opportunity for the subsidence of fundamental differences. It is fortunate, therefore, that the leaders of the community have to a considerable extent already fallen into a certain topographical segregation or separation, and in many parts of India the Mahomedan aristocracies are so distributed geographically as to be able to avoid a collision with their Hindoo rivals. It appears desirable that the British Government should extend a helping hand to assist this natural tendency.

The lower orders would remain unaffected by such a separation, and to the bulk of the people the difficulties of assimilation do not apply. The delta of Bengal, for instance, is peopled for the most part by quiet and inoffensive races, whether Mussulman or Hindoo, between whom, from long association, a close affinity exists. The followers of Islam, who constitute an undoubted majority of the population, differ little in language, customs, or occupation from the older inhabitants of the country. In other parts of India, Mahomedans are more or less of foreign extraction, and there is a strain of Arab or Persian blood in their veins. But in Eastern Bengal the Mahomedans are comparatively recent converts. They are for the most part one and indivisible from the Hindoos among whom they dwell. They are of the same race, and live together on friendly and affectionate terms. In this division of the country the difficulty does not present itself, and no trace of hostility between Hindoos and Mahomedans has ever been found under normal conditions. There never was a trace of it until the elements of strife were kindled by the unfortunate partition of the Bengal Province, and attempts were made to fan them into a flame by the injudicious attitude of a Lieutenant-Governor whose example is not likely to be followed by his successors. It is the merest justice to accord this credit to the Indian Government that the sinister policy of "divide and rule," so often dinned into their ears, has almost invariably been recognised as dangerous and unwise.

In other parts of India it will generally be found that the Mahomedans are still, as they were under their own dynasty, the principal members of the community, and that they have established among themselves a certain exclusiveness from the Hindoos among whom it is their lot to live. They have their own traditions and their own aspirations. It is largely owing to the demands of their religious creed that they are less inclined than the Hindoos to adapt themselves to an English education, and they have in consequence in no small measure been crowded out of the offices of emolument and position they once enjoyed. The Indian Government have, with characteristic impartiality, favoured neither race nor creed among the subject populations. Employment in the public service has drifted, therefore, into the hands of those most qualified by their education to discharge official duties. This has been a chronic source of irritation among Mahomedans, and has tended to prevent their co-operation with their Hindoo compatriots.

The late Sir Syed Ahmed Khan was the leader of the Mahomedans. He devoted himself to the encouragement of their education, and gave a great stimulus in this direction by the establishment of the Mahomedan Anglo-Oriental College at Allygurh. His sympathies in the first instance were with the National Congress movement. Mahomedans and Hindoos were, he said, the two eyes of India—injure the one and you injure the other. At Gurdaspore, on 27th January 1884, he said: "We should try to become one heart and soul, and act in unison; if united we can support each other; if not, the effect of one against the other will tend to the destruction and downfall of both." And again, on 3rd February 1884, at Lahore, he spoke in very remarkable terms: "I assure you that the Bengalees are the only people in our country whom we can properly be proud of, and it is only due to them that knowledge, liberty, and patriotism have progressed in our country. I can truly say that they are the head and crown of all the communities of Hindustan . . . . In the word 'nation' I include both Hindoos and Mahomedans, because that is the only meaning which I can attach to it." This language was, however, in complete contrast to that which he afterwards employed. As soon as he came to perceive that the Government was unfriendly to the Congress movement, he changed his attitude. His acute sense of political opportunism was prompt to seize the practical advantage which would accrue to the interests of a minority which dissociated itself from any political demonstration distasteful to the authorities. He therefore threw the whole of his influence into the scale against the growing national movement. He counselled his co-religionists to refrain from political agitation, and as a body they followed his advice.

Nevertheless, many prominent Mahomedans

have always adhered to the Congress, and on many occasions the deliberations of the Provincial and National Congresses have been presided over by Mahomedans. New ideas have sprung into life since the generation of Sir Syed Ahmed. The Hindoo community is at the present moment watching with the deepest interest the political ferment, the outcome of intellectual progress, which has set in at Allygurh. The attitude of Hindoos has never been antagonistic to Mahomedan aspirations. Mahomedan interests find no more ardent advocate than in the columns of the Hindoo press. The attitude of Mahomedans has become more and more responsive to Hindoo sentiment. The Aga Khan of Bombay, who was the mouthpiece of the recent Mahomedan deputation to the Viceroy, and Nawab Syed Mahomed, of Madras, who is a member of the Viceroy's Legislative Council, were careful to explain that their attitude was sympathetic with, and not hostile to, Hindoo or Indian aspirations. There was a careful avoidance in this address to the Viceroy of any reference to the dissensions which have been temporarily stirred up in Eastern Bengal. There are evidences in this deputation of a closer relation between Mahomedans and Hindoos.

There are signs of a common feeling arising in favour of the united co-operation of the two great communities. Why should differences of race and creed be allowed to dominate the larger and vital interests of India? Why should they not subside in an harmonious and successful effort to combine forces, too long conflicting, into a brotherly movement in the interests of their common country? Mutual trust, a frank interchange of views, a sense of hearty communion and co-operation, a desire for unity for the achievement of common ends and objects, without which no real or lasting advance can ever be accomplished—these are the new ideas of the rising generation, not less of Mahomedans than of Hindoos.

The future of the European settlers and of the Eurasian community demands a similar but somewhat easier solution. The tendency of Eurasians to imitate the attitude of Europeans in regard to Indians is a source of growing disturbance, inasmuch as their claims to social supremacy cannot be admitted by the more strictly called native community. These claims arise only from blood and language relations with British-born subjects, who, however, on their part, hold the Eurasians at a distance in consequence of their relationship with the natives. Excluded on both sides, their condition is extremely anomalous, and if England were to abandon India it is probable that as a class they would sink to the level of the Mahomedan proletariat. But if England does not break off from India, as we know she will not, it seems that the welfare of the Eurasians as well as of Europeans can be best secured by the formation of separate little settlements at suitable localities, resembling the free cities of Germany or the city republics of Venice and Genoa. Such cities would then contain the European and Eurasian community who may choose to reside in the country. This is a state of things which is now, in fact, actually growing up. All the important civil and military stations in India comprise what is called a European quarter, and the municipal administration of such places is a source of endless misunderstanding between the native and Anglo-Indian populations. Complete separation, both by geographical limits and political institutions, is apparently the only means of putting an end to irritation which in times of political trouble may easily become a source of serious danger. Their protection, if protection were necessary, will be afforded by the prestige and power of England. But it is not necessary.

It has been acutely suggested by one of my Indian friends—a friend to whom I am indebted for other suggestions on this subject—that the alarm so often raised by Anglo-Indians on the ground of hostility from the natives means nothing more than a consciousness of their own hostile inclinations towards the natives. Indians may be irrational and uncompromisingly exclusive, but they are not aggressive. And the alarms of the Anglo-Indians, seemingly so innocent and so entirely on the defensive, are designed only to rouse the sympathies of Englishmen at home, so that they may send forth succour which the Anglo-Indians know very well will serve them also for purposes of aggression. Even if all military support from England were withdrawn, the withdrawal would not be injurious to Anglo-Indians, who, when conveniently located in separate places and with separate political constitutions, would be constrained in their own self-interest to adopt a more conciliatory demeanour towards the people of the country.

Turning now to the question of foreign invasion, on which I must say a few words, I think most persons will be found to agree that there need be no apprehension of such invasion from Asiatic Powers ; if there be, it may be presumed that the various States and free cities would be strong enough to resist any attack. But it will be alleged that the real fear of foreign invasion is from European Powers, and probably from Russia. There are persons to whom Russia is a constant dread, a kind of demon of infinite capacity, possessed by a malignant and unceasing desire to wrest India from our hands. It is a curious phenomenon this prejudice against Russia; but it is a prejudice as baseless as it is hard to explain. The Russophobist labours under a strange hallucination, which has existed without intermission for nearly a century, and even now, when we have seen the annihilation of Russia's forces in Manchuria, has been by no means dispelled. Yet we have on record the views of the Tsar himself. In the *Memoirs of the late Prince Hohenlohe* an account is given of a discussion between the Chancellor and the present Tsar Nicholas, in the course of which Prince Hohenlohe took occasion to observe that the English attached the utmost importance to their supremacy in South Africa because, in their fear of one day losing India, they desired to keep consolation at hand in the shape of an empire in Africa. To which the Tsar rejoined: "Yes; but who is going to take India from them? We are not so stupid as to pursue a design of that sort."

I, for my part, believe with Mr Bright "that Russia has no more idea of crossing the frontier of India into the Indian Empire than we have of crossing the frontier of India and invading the Asiatic possessions of Russia." With Lord Salisbury, I would advise the victims of a baseless scare to buy large-sized maps, and learn how insuperable are the obstacles which Nature has placed between the land of the Czar and the Indian dominions of the British Crown. With Lord Beaconsfield, "I think that from the period of the conquest of Tashkend, some ten years ago,[1] everyone must have felt that it was almost inevitable that all of these khanates would be conquered by Russia. Some gentlemen think that this advance of Russia ought to be nipped in the bud. But nipping it in the bud means that the English Power should have proceeded beyond our Indian boundary, and should have entered on a most hazardous and, I should say, most unwise struggle. I am not of that sort which views the advance of Russia in Asia with deep misgivings." These remarks of Lord Beaconsfield indicate with prescient sagacity that the

[1] This was said in 1876.

simplest, safest, and cheapest way of solving the so-called Central Asian difficulty is by trusting to the natural defences of India as the best protection of that country. For it is true that the obstacles which Nature has placed between the land of the Tsar and the Indian dominions of the British Crown are insuperable. Aggression on the part of Russia into India would be as suicidal in her case, as the aggression on the part of England towards Herat would infallibly result in the destruction of any army despatched thither. War, of course, may result from the folly and wickedness of the rulers of either country; the war parties in England and Russia alike are a menace to the progress and prosperity of mankind; but the invasion of India by Russia is one of the most improbable of contingencies.

Mr Balfour, in his speech[1] in the House of Commons on Imperial Defence, has also done much to place matters in a proper light. He has pointed out that not only is the invasion of India "no part of a scheme of the Russian Government," but that "no surprise and no rush is possible in India," and that "India cannot be taken by assault." Transport and supply are a physical impossibility without

[1] On 11th May 1905.

railways, and the construction of railways across Afghanistan would be the labour of years. "The Afghans are not likely to welcome these railways in their passes"; that was another wise reminder, and the opponents of a forward policy have no reason to object to the declaration that if any attempt is made to build a railway, in connection with the Russian strategic railways, in the territory of Afghanistan, it ought to be considered an act of direct aggression upon England. "Railways in Afghanistan," Mr Balfour hastened to add, "shall only be made in time of war"; and although the point was not raised in the debate, it follows from this that England, in her turn, must refrain from railway interference.

No one has welcomed the enunciation of this policy with more cordiality than the people of India. None will pray more fervently that it may never be repudiated. Their minds were never agitated by the conflict of opinion, which loomed so largely in the public eye of this country, between Lord Kitchener and Lord Curzon. A plague on both your houses, was the Indian commentary on this dispute. *Delirant reges, plectuntur Achivi.* It is against a militant and aggressive policy in all its aspects that they unreservedly protest; against pyrotechnics in Tibet, in Beluchistan, on the Persian Gulf, and generally beyond the frontier, which have contributed so greatly to the increase of military expenditure. They rejoice at every discouragement of Imperialism in Asia. Mr Balfour was considering the matter from the British point of view. But the adoption of his conclusions cannot fail to have an important bearing upon taxation and expenditure in India. It must logically lead to reduction of expenditure on the North-West frontier, where enormous sums of money have been and are being poured out like water. A nail has been driven into the coffin of the forward frontier policy. And all who are concerned with peace, retrenchment, and reform in India will recall the extravagance and suffering which that policy has involved.

The safest guarantee of British rule in India is a contented people. Our surest safeguard is the existence of a federated and grateful nation, to which the largest concession of political rights has been accorded and the amplest justice rendered. Russia would be as powerless against a united India as Europe has shown itself to be against China. Professor Seeley has shown that in the proper sense of the word India was never conquered by England. The people of India never united to oppose the

English. Whenever one Indian State has been overthrown, it has almost invariably been with the help of some other Indian State. There was no Indian nation, and there has therefore been no real English conquest of India. No foreign Power could conquer India if she were a true nation. The present form of British administration cannot survive the fulfilment of those national tendencies which we have ourselves brought into existence. But India is bound to England, as England is to India. The future of India will be a federation of independent States cemented together by the authority of England. India so constituted will afford from its own resources the most powerful check against aggression for all time. The close connection of England with India, the attitude of the foster-mother country under the proposed Colonial relations, and of the free cities, which must always be English in tone and spirit, will not only tend to prevent a short-sighted jealousy, but will materially strengthen the United States of India in presenting an unbroken front of opposition to a common foe.

In any case it may be argued that it would not be difficult for England on the withdrawal of her own standing army to secure treaty rights for India from the European Powers.

Such rights would be the easier to negotiate for if it were seen that England were honestly giving up its policy of self-aggrandisement. The evidence of honesty of purpose so recognised would inexpressibly benefit the cause of peace and future progress.

THE SOCIAL AND MORAL CRISIS

It has been justly said that the India of the present is no more like the India of Lord Ellenborough than the England of to-day is like the England of Queen Anne. This remark is equally true in respect of moral, social, and intellectual advancement as in regard to material affairs. But, morally and socially at least, the change is far greater than this analogy would imply. In England there has been evolution, not revolution. The change has been the result of natural spontaneous progress brought about by the action of internal forces. In India the change has been artificial and forced from without. It is the product of the relationship between two civilisations at an unequal stage of development in immediate contact with one another. The question in India, therefore, is not one of progress only ; the movement, so far as it has gone, is revolution pure and simple : in other words, it is the introduction of the complex machinery of Western civilisation into the simple society of the East.

The moving spirit of this revolution is English education. Under its solvent influence the old organisations are crumbling up, and the Indian races have entered upon a long career of transition preparatory to the establishment of a new order. The immediate inevitable result of this is disturbance. Our admiration for Western civilisation would be blind indeed if we were not able to see that grave evils must inevitably attend upon its transplantation to Indian soil. The actual Hindooism of the present has behind it a polytheistic past of thirty centuries or more, which must mould and colour its future, whatever the form it may hereafter take. The effect of English education has been to break this continuity. The habits and opinions of the people are modified, and even their mode of life is changed, but the hereditary tendencies by which the progress of the race must ultimately be determined are left untouched. There is no power of guidance or consolidation. It is possible for Government to exercise an ennobling influence upon a people with whom it is completely homogeneous. But where this homogeneity does not exist, the influence of the governors is of a very different character. It is not possible to effect permanent good by educational establishments which are in the hands of an alien power, and therefore of men who cannot fully sympathise with the wants of the people. It is not possible to successfully disseminate Western ideas through an official channel. The Roman prefects of old were all unequal to the task of Christianising the empire ; far less is the de-polytheising of India a task reserved for officials to undertake. Such a change can only be effected by voluntary efforts, partly foreign and partly indigenous, the doctrine coming in its main features from the West, but being moulded into appropriate forms by Eastern intellects.

It is certain that the regenerating doctrine must arise in the West. The vanguard of Humanity is in the West ; and the development of the race everywhere being due to the same fundamental laws, must correspond in its main features with the earlier development of its most advanced portion. But if we look at the West as it actually is, we find a state of utter confusion in every department of human energy. Nations, Churches, and Classes are at war with one another, and disunited among themselves. It is a serious symptom of insufficiency that there should be found among us those who hope to establish a national organisation upon the disorganised forces of Christendom. It is even more deplorable that any should advocate the wholesale importation into India of European civilisation in its most material and anarchical form, without any moral safeguards. The present anarchy which prevails in Europe characterises the transitional epoch between the repressive policy of the old Catholic *régime* and that healthier policy of the future which is destined to rest upon a basis of a stable and progressive public opinion. But what does such anarchy become when transplanted to the East? There it is the natural product of no such period of transition; it is a disintegrating force intruding into an alien order of things; it is an agent of destruction, of which the disastrous effects will have to be carefully eliminated at some future period. The West must be itself united before it can expect to produce a salutary influence upon the less advanced populations. Any present movement is premature. Such as was the dominion of Rome in the East, such must be that of Great Britain in India; and with England, as with Rome, the simple keeping of the peace must be the main object. The principal end of our government should be to maintain the *status quo* until modifications can be introduced which shall enable the passage from the old to the new order to be accomplished with the least perceptible disturbance.

We may be thankful that our action affects at present only a small portion of the community, and that the vast bulk of the people of India is still unmoved by any of the moral or civilising influences which contact with the missionaries or the efforts of the Department of Public Instruction might be expected to impart. Nothing but disaster could ensue from unsettling the beliefs and prejudices of the multitude at too early a stage of its development. It will be time enough when the *élite* of the Hindoo community is thoroughly initiated into the civilisation of the West to consider how changes can be best introduced among the masses of the people.

Still more cause for thankfulness is there in the fact that the preliminary period of the revolution, during which the educational machinery has been under the direct control of a foreign Government, is drawing to a close. Official interference was unavoidable in the first instance—in no other way could a beginning have been made—but the educational movement in India now stands in need of no such stimulus. The sense of utter dependence on Government for support has given way before the progressive, enlightened, and independent spirit to which English education itself has given birth. The cry for English education which rings through all the Presidencies is sufficient evidence that there exists in India, as well as in Europe, a worthy instinct among the people, a popular craving for education demanding satisfaction, and not an obstinacy requiring that it should be thrust upon them. National schools and colleges have been established. Educational institutions, unaided by Government or by missionary societies, independent in the strictest sense of the word, are now flourishing with hundreds of English-speaking scholars, and set an example in instruction, discipline, and moral training which the older schools and colleges may well envy.

It is in matters of education more than any other that the people of the country have become ripe for local self-government. The fact that large and high-class educational institutions can be effectually managed by Indian agency alone no longer admits of doubt. Systematic education is already falling into the hands of private enterprise. The time has come for the Government to transfer its educational endowments to the custody of those who have been educated in them. The present system of University administration, which is most unsatisfactory in all respects, should be reconstituted on a representative basis. The policy of Lord Curzon, which knitted together still tighter the bonds of official control, is absolutely retrograde. It has been condemned by every section of Indian opinion ; and though it may temporarily prevail, it will be as evanescent as it is unsound. It is only through the educated members of the Indian community that it is possible to guide the people at large so as to bridge over the period of disorder with the least disturbance. It is reserved for them to introduce modifications with due regard to the antecedents which must always powerfully affect the environment in which they are placed. The problem of grafting Western ideas on to an Oriental stock is now ready for solution in the only way in which a successful solution is possible—by means of Orientals who, having been thoroughly imbued, under our present system of education, with a knowledge of Western civilisation, have at the same time not lost sight of the traditions of their past.

It is no longer possible for the Government to exercise any beneficial interference in this direction. Its function is exhausted, and its chief end in view should be to maintain order while the remaining period of transition is in the hands of those who may be able to control the movement. The true attitude, for some time to come at least, should be one of conservation and the encouragement of a system of protection. Its wisest policy will be to refrain from any action which leads directly to collision with the old theocratic organisation. The old Hindoo polytheism is a present basis of moral order, and rests upon foundations so plastic that it can be moulded into the most diverse forms, adapting itself equally to the intellect of the subtle metaphysician and to the emotions of the unlettered peasant. It combines in itself all the elements of intensity, regularity, and permanence. Its chief attribute is stability. The system of caste, far from being the source of all the troubles which can be traced in Hindoo society, has rendered the most important services in the past, and still continues to sustain order and solidarity. The admirable order of Hindooism is too valuable to be rashly sacrificed before any Moloch of progress. Better is order without progress, if that were possible, than progress with disorder. Hindooism is still vigorous, and the strength of its metaphysical subtlety and wide range of influence are yet instinct with life. In the future its distinctive conceptions will be preserved and incorporated into a higher faith ; but at present we are utterly incapable of replacing it by a religion which shall at once reflect the national life, and be competent to form a nucleus round which the love and reverence of its votaries may cluster.

The task now before us is to preserve order as far as may be practicable, and not to excite unnecessary disturbance. This duty is paramount in its political aspect, but it is, if possible, even more incumbent on us in its social and moral relations. The existing social order demands, therefore, our first attention, and to this end I can find nothing more essential than a careful study and correct appreciation of the Hindoo caste system. That system has its defects undoubtedly, but they are defects more than counterbalanced by the services it renders. Those reformers who are in the habit of describing caste as the root of all evils in Hindoo society overlook the impossibility of uprooting an institution which has taken such a firm hold on the popular mind. They forget that the attempt to abolish caste, if successful, would be attended with the most dangerous consequences, unless some powerful religious influence were brought to bear upon the people in its place. They forget also that caste is still stronger as a social than as a religious institution, and that many a man who has entirely lost his belief in his religion is zealous and tenacious of his position as a high-caste man, and scrupulously performs all customary rites and ceremonies. Caste is now the framework which knits together Hindoo society; it is the link which maintains the existing religious system of Hindooism in its present order. The problem of the future is not to destroy caste, but to modify it, to preserve its distinctive conceptions, and to gradually place them upon a social instead of a supernatural basis.

The Christian missionary condemns caste because he finds it hard to destroy a priesthood which receives a support from the people when nothing in the shape of spiritual assistance is rendered in return. The British administrator condemns the institution because he cannot, on account of it, override the internal discipline of a subject community, and finds himself ranked by them, for all his authority, with their veriest outcasts. I remember well the impression created in my own mind on my first arrival in India, when, on walking out in the evening with a Brahmin subordinate, the Hindoos whom we might meet would accost me with the respectful gesture they will always accord to official rank, while they would prostrate themselves and rub their foreheads in the dust before my companion. To him they rendered a genuine obeisance; to me they showed a sign of artificial respect only. The sense of official relationship was entirely swallowed up by the stronger feeling of social subordination. It is not only the lower orders that are inspired by this feeling; all are affected by it. Caste still exercises a predominant influence among all classes of the community. Educated Hindoos are puzzled to make out what they owe to their society, and why they render to caste their tribute of submission when there is nothing to compel their obedience. Nevertheless, the institution is as powerful among those who disregard many of its rules as it was with their fathers who rigidly observed them all. They find it as hard to bear excommunication themselves, and are as disposed to inflict that punishment upon wrongdoers of their community, as was the case with their ancestors in the past. They find it as desirable to cling to their caste-fellows, despite many disagreeable features in their life and character, as their predecessors may have done. Even those who are outside the pale of Hindoo caste seem anxious to organise an institution resembling caste among themselves. The Eurasian community seems to have already formed into a caste, and the native converts to Christianity, as well as the more self-assertive portion of the Brahmo community, appear to be in the course of forming into new castes. Even a Khalsa Sikh will be found to assume an attitude of marked respect towards Brahmins, and to entertain the most delicate scruples on the subject of caste. Even Mahomedans have been so far infected that they have broken up into separate castes with the *jus connubii* as distinct as it is amongst Hindoos.

Caste is thus the existing basis of social order, as the Brahminical polytheism is of Hindoo morality. Supplemented by such sister institutions as the joint family and the village community (both of which are also in transition and have been greatly changed), it has already been subjected to modifications, and is destined to be still further modified by the external influences which are brought to bear on it. Its future must, however, remain a mere speculation so long as the Hindoo nation cannot assume the responsibility of working out its own social evolution. In their present condition the Hindoos cannot possibly have an ideal of their own. Bereft of political independence, their ideas of collective action cannot bear that impress of sound logic and morality which collective action alone can impart to them. A considerable degree of unity in thought and action has lately been established in political matters, and it may be hoped, therefore, that there will shortly be a similar manifestation in regard to moral and social questions. The problem is a difficult one, and in proportion to its difficulty will be the merit and the reward of those who succeed in solving it. There is neither difficulty nor merit in merely cutting the Gordian knot, which is the method of procedure pursued by Government. The necessary changes must be wrought by the people themselves, arising from national aspirations and emanating from a spontaneous impulse. The changes effected by an alien and benevolently despotic administration are spasmodic and artificial, and they cannot be of permanent value because they are not spontaneous.

The truth is that the moral and social reformation of India, as of every other country, if it is to be effective, must result from the action of internal forces. Its tendencies must be moulded by the accumulated influences of the past and by the direct action of the present. It cannot disconnect itself from the associations which have grown up around the family for generations. It must begin among the domestic *lares* and *penates*. And this is why civilisation through a foreign government, the popularisation of Western ideas through official insistence, a system of education through officials employed under the Department of Public Instruction, must always fail. Education will never be in a healthy condition so long as the teaching of the home is at utter variance with the teaching of the school or college. Anyone who is acquainted with the conditions of an ordinary Hindoo family at its home must have been struck with the bewildering contrast between the domestic environment of the young Hindoo, amidst which his active life is spent, and the intellectual atmosphere he breathes during his college hours. The domestic life of the Hindoo is indeed in itself not more immoral than that of a European home. Far from it ; there is so much misconception on this point that it is desirable to state what the facts actually are. The affection of Hindoos for the various members of the family group is a praiseworthy and distinctive feature of national character, evinced not in sentiment only, but in practical manifestations of enduring charity ; the devotion of a parent to a child, and of children to parents, is most touching. The normal social relations of a Hindoo family, knit together by ties of affection, rigid in chastity, and controlled by the public opinion of neighbouring elders and caste, command our admiration, and in many respects afford an example we should do well to follow. There is nothing radically wrong in the young Hindoo's home associations. But the life he leads does present a painful contradiction where, to take an ordinary type, the family idols are tended by the mother and the other female members of the family at sunrise and sunset with flowers and ablutions and ceremonial observances; and in the meantime the midday occupation of the student consists in analysing, it may be, Milton's *Areopagitica*, a favourite text-book in my day, or some other scathing exposition of priestcraft and idolatry. The Professors of the Educational Department deliver their lectures and discourse on Milton or Mill in the same spirit as a magistrate dispenses justice in his cutchery. They do their official duty, but they make no attempt to exert a moral influence over their pupils, to form their sentiments and habits, or to control and guide their passions. The moral character is left to be wholly moulded by the associations amidst which the young are placed at home, without any endeavour to modify or improve it. There is thus a great gulf fixed between the relative position of the intellectual and of the moral culture. Collegiate impressions are at present, like a tinselled outdoor decoration, discarded by their possessor as a superfluity in private. And in the majority of cases they are, at all times, apparent rather than real; for though the educated natives lose their belief in Hindooism as an intellectual system, it still continues in a marked degree to mould their social and moral prejudices. The result is an anarchy for which the Government is responsible and which it is powerless to remedy. A tendency to look to the State for assistance, a disposition to exaggerate the power of political action over social events, is natural ; but while in some cases, no doubt, the evils felt fall legitimately within the scope of politics, in others—and these are the vast majority—the Government is powerless to effect a cure, or can at best employ but palliative measures. Government can do little more than hold the purse and keep the peace, and put down practices like *suttee*, which are positively murderous ; but even in a case like this, it cannot eradicate the sentiment upon which the practice depends.

The situation is now one of extreme social anarchy ; and although the disturbance is not widespread, but prevails only among a limited section of the people, the mere existence of a disorganised class within the community is in itself no small evil. I am not blind to the defects of this class. I count among its members innumerable friends of sterling merit, and of a high order of probity and ability. No English official has been more indebted than I have been for Indian aid and co-operation most generously accorded at all times. I would be the last to speak unkindly of friends, colleagues, and comrades in a distant country. And yet I cannot but observe that the class as a whole labours under defects which are not less serious because they are the result of circumstances over which it has little or no control. The class is educated—highly educated as compared with the mass of the people: who can wonder that it should be conceited? The class is debarred from holding the highest offices under Government: who can wonder that it should be discontented? The class is an artificial and exotic product: who can wonder that it should be internally torn by a life of self-contradiction more or less in almost every individual instance?

Such are the penalties which the early pioneers of English education in India have had to pay for the knowledge and power they have acquired. The strength of national associations and social sentiment has fortunately sustained them for the most part with their own personal character untainted by demoralisation. It is true that they have not altogether escaped the vices of the West; but the virtues of the West, which they have successfully assimilated, immeasurably turn the scale. The difficulties under which they labour are occasioned by the abrupt departures from old habit and custom, the domestic discords, the social dissensions, the religious confusion, the tenebrous rationalism which insufficiently supplies the place of a belief in the old theology, the bitter and increasing sense of political discontent, the growing irritation arising from the existence of racial disability and prejudice, and the very life of concealment, and even of self-deception, which as individuals they are so often compelled to lead. The gravity of these difficulties it is almost impossible to exaggerate.

Enough, however, of such criticism. It is not my object to depreciate the importance of passing events. I have shown no desire to extenuate the difficulties through which India must pass during this revolutionary transition, or to minimise the troubles of the existing crisis. It is certain that when the State endeavours to impart higher instruction, and thereby, as is implied, to direct and mould the national mind, it deviates from its proper sphere, and inflicts injury upon intellectual and moral progress. The unavoidable symptoms of social disorder created by such interference are readily recognisable, and have often been the occasion of unfriendly comment. But when I bring the evil done into comparison with the good; when I take into consideration not only the actual benefits received, but the potential good which must ultimately extend to the whole population; when I recall that English education has burst upon the natives of India for a period of two generations only; when I observe its effects on all sides and weigh them in the balance, I cannot hesitate to affirm that, notwithstanding drawbacks of all and whatever kind, the dissemination of Western ideas has proved of inestimable advantage to the country.

The beneficial tendency of this revolution is undoubted. In ever-widening circles it must gradually extend among classes of society at present undisturbed; and as natural forces are encouraged to take the place of artificial development, the demoralisation inseparable from change will become less apparent. And if its injurious tendency is also undoubted, it must be remembered that periods of transition are always accompanied by more or less disturbance. To me, indeed, it seems more noticeable that the community affected should have passed in so large a measure unscathed through the ordeal, than that it should have been demoralised so far as to allow in some respects the vices of Europe to supplant virtues of a distinctly Oriental type.

If we may observe in the minds of many educated natives an undisguised contempt for the simple faith of their forefathers; if we must admit the existence of a tendency to exaggerate the value of modern at the expense of ancient achievements; if we cannot deny that one effect of our education has been to undermine the social feelings of attachment, obedience, reverence for age, and respect for ancestors—if these are evils which English education has encouraged—I make bold to say that among the leaders of the Indian community and among the mass of the people who follow their guidance there is little or no sympathy with these tendencies. The vast majority of Hindoo thinkers have formed themselves into a party of reaction against the voice of a crude and empirical rationalism which seeks only to decry the social monuments raised in ancient times by Brahmin theocrats and legislators, to vilify the past in order to glorify the present, and to sing the shallow glories of an immature civilisation with praises never accorded to the greatest triumphs of humanity in the past. The innate conservatism of the nation is beyond the power of any foreign civilisation to shatter. The stability of the Hindoo character could have shown itself in no way more conspicuously than by the wisdom with which it has bent itself before the irresistible rush of Western thought, and has still preserved amidst all the havoc of destruction an underlying current of religious sentiment, and a firm conviction that social and moral order can only rest upon a religious basis.

THE RELIGIOUS TENDENCIES OF INDIA

ONE of the earliest and best established principles of British administration in India is that of religious neutrality. The Government of India, as between its subjects and itself, does not assume the truth or falsehood of any religion. It allows perfect freedom and liberty to the professors of all creeds. In accordance with this principle, the various provisional phases of religious speculation (the intuitive outcome of Western thought) which are to be found in more or less restless activity among the educated classes of India have not been subjected to any form of official interference. The Government is, perhaps, open to reproach for using its power unduly to advance Christianity when it supports bishops, archdeacons, and a considerable staff of Anglican and Presbyterian chaplains out of revenues almost wholly raised from Hindoos and Mahomedans. There are cases in which high officials have injudiciously identified themselves with the promotion and propaganda of their Christian creed. Still, it is undoubtedly the case that, like the Roman prefects of old, our Indian administrators have in general been careless about spiritual matters. The Government has, broadly speaking, exercised no influence whatever to induce the natives to become Christians, and the natives have responded to this indifference by showing no desire whatever to become converts to the State religion. When Hindooism ceases to be a living power in the minds of the young men who frequent our English schools and colleges, Christianity rarely, if ever, takes its place. The very fact of its profession by the foreign rulers of the country has been represented to me by Indian gentlemen as a valid reason for their aversion to it.

The strong missionary body, which is more of an educating than a proselytising force, offers some substitute for the beliefs which it destroys. Our State colleges are content with chaos; their results are subversive only ; the old belief is thrown off, the consequent disturbance issues in no real substitute, and the mental and moral state suffers from the negation. The missionary scheme does contemplate the establishment of an order. It is to the credit of the missionaries that they have ever held the right end in view, viz., the substitution of a definite social and religious conception for the old Hindoo polity, the downfall of which they foresaw. In the main they have done a good work, and done it bravely. But their failure has been complete. Far be it from me to depreciate the wonderful moral efficacy of Catholicism and the remarkable example of self-sacrifice it once set in a portion of Southern India. But a retrospect of the past no longer presents a promise of any successful proselytism in the future. Wherever there is a highly organised religious creed, Christianity fails to make conversions on any large scale. It is absolutely powerless when brought face to face with Islam; and among Hindoos its influence is confined almost exclusively to the very lowest classes,[1] where the mental development has

[1] It has been shrewdly remarked by a competent Catholic writer on this subject, that "at the very outset of missionary enterprise, the progress of Christianity among the lower castes only, tended to augment tenfold the repugnance and hostility of the Brahmins and other high-caste Hindoos. It cannot be too often insisted on that caste is a social as well as a religious distinction. Christianity thus not only appeared in the eyes of Hindoos as a religious innovation, but as the creed of socialism and license which allied itself with all that was lowest and most infamous in the country. In propagating opinions of any kind it is always hazardous to ignore the natural leaders of a community, and attempt to win over the multitude without their co-operation." —*Dublin Quarterly Review*, October 1868.

not advanced much beyond the earliest stage. Though here and there an educated native may have been brought to Christianity, the educated natives, as a body, have not been slow to perceive that the intellect of Europe is drifting away from the traditional religion. Whatever change may eventually be effected, the change from Hindooism to Christianity is perhaps the most improbable; the people will not accept it.

The remarks of Dr Congreve on the prospects of Christianity in India, and on the relations between Christianity and Hindooism and Islam, are so apposite that I cannot do better than quote them in this place. He writes:—

We have two religious systems to deal with in India, the Mahomedan and the Brahminical. Both are yet powerful—on neither can we make any impression. If in his contact with Brahminism the missionary puts forward the philosophical side of Christianity, the subtle mind of the Brahmin delights in the combat, and meets him with a counter-philosophy. There is matter for endless dispute, but there is no result. If, more wisely advised, the missionary rests on the simple statements of Christianity, on the facts of its history and its appeals to the conscience of men, he spares himself personally the annoyance of defeat in argument, or the pain of seeing his arguments make no impression, but for his cause the effect is the same. For the religious system of India leaves its worshippers no sense of want, that primary condition of the acceptance of a new religion. The contest is not such as it was with the polytheistic systems of Greece and Rome, which were profoundly undermined by the philosophic culture of the educated, by the moral dissatisfaction of the multitude. In India such would not seem to be the case; and when you add to the absence of this the force of traditional associations and long organisation, the power of which was tested in the case of the Greek and Roman world, and not broken but by four centuries and a barbarian conquest, you have then the measure of the missionary's difficulties in dealing with Brahminism; you may form an estimate of the hopelessness of his task.

For the second great religious system with which we are in contact, little need be said. The verdict of history is definite and unimpeachable. On Mahomedanism, Christianity has made no impression, has tacitly renounced the attempt to make any. The rival Monotheisms met in the Middle Ages. The issue of the struggle was not doubtful. Greek Christianity succumbed. Latin Christianity waged successfully a defensive war. More than this it was unable to accomplish. Each of the rivals claims for itself an exclusive possession of the religious belief of mankind. Both alike are rejected by the other. They rest side by side, convincing monuments of the exaggeration of their respective claims.

Again, Colonel Osborn, speaking of the missionary failure from another point of view, observes with equal truth :—

> The chief obstacle which besets the missionary is that occasioned by the peculiar relationship which exists between Englishmen and natives. The English are not merely the rulers of the country, but rulers in whose inner life, as individuals, the people are of no account—that is to say, the English in India form no attachments, no friendships with the people of the country. A few among them may associate with the natives from a sense of duty, but for their mental and moral needs their own countrymen are sufficient, and not one Englishman in a thousand, when the hour comes of leaving India for good, is sensible of a wrench, of a void being created in his life by the separation from any native whom he has known. No greater obstacle in the way of missionary work can be conceived than a state of mind such as this. It denotes the want of that touch of nature which makes the whole world kin, and yet it is a defect from which the English missionary is, of necessity, as little exempt as the English official. . . . . Contrast this attitude of aloofness with the feelings of the Apostle Paul towards individual members of the churches which he had founded, and we shall find little difficulty in understanding why Christianity in India does not spread and develop as in the days of imperial Rome.

To these remarks I only wish to add that there is now within my own observation an increasing opposition to Christianity among the educated classes, a greater repugnance to its doctrines, and a more effective desire to prevent it spreading in any way among the rising generation. The spread of education has enabled the people to bind together with more cohesion and unity against a form of proselytism they so much dislike, and conversions to Christianity, otherwise than among the very lowest classes of the people, who are attracted to Christianity because it raises their position in the social scale, among famine remnants who have been taken over in large numbers by missionary bodies, and among the aboriginal tribes, are far less frequent than was formerly the case. During my long residence in India, I can scarcely recall the conversion of a respectable Indian gentleman to Christianity.

Nevertheless, although the educated Hindoos do not become Christians, they do not as a rule get rid of their belief in a supreme government. The Hindoo mind naturally runs in a religious groove of thought, and recoils from any solution of its present difficulties which does not arise from the past religious history of the nation. And therefore the vast majority of Hindoo thinkers do not venture to reject the supernatural from their belief. They adopt Theism in some form or other, and endeavour in this way to give permanence and vitality to what they conceive to be the religion of their ancient scriptures. At the same time they manage to reconcile with this teaching the ceremonial observances of a strictly orthodox Polytheism. They argue that these rites are embedded in the traditions and customs of the people, that they are harmless in themselves, and that their observance tends to bridge over the chasm which otherwise separates the educated classes from the bulk of the population. Their action is thus animated by a spirit of large-hearted tolerance. And there is nothing in it inconsistent with itself. For there is no direct antagonism between a belief in one supreme being ruling over a number of inferior powers, and a belief in several co-ordinate deities, each exercising sovereignty within certain vaguely defined limits. At best, however, their attitude is but a compromise between Rationalism and Hindooism. It is liable to misconception and abuse. And therefore it is distasteful to certain ardent minds which revolt altogether from compromise, and deem it obligatory to purge themselves from all taint of idolatry or superstition by entering a solemn protest against the popular creed, which they regard as at once false and mischievous. It is to such minds that Brahmoism owes its origin and development.

I have no prejudice against the Brahmos as a body ; on the contrary, I have the highest personal respect for many of their number, and especially for their distinguished leaders, who have been endowed with no ordinary share of those gifts which enable their possessors to become teachers of the people. I have been myself a witness at the Brahmo services of the remarkable degree of religious intensity of which the Hindoo mind is capable. I have no question that Brahmoism has proved a haven to many who would otherwise have been cast adrift upon the troubled waves of doubt, and that it has afforded them a religion which satisfies their aspirations and ennobles their mode of life. But I find it impossible to regard Brahmoism as a definite belief. It is altogether an esoteric doctrine, not materially distinguishable from the Theism or Unitarianism of Europe. It appeals to the individual, and requires not only a minute process of self-examination, but also a concurrence among individuals in their interpretations of self-consciousness. Its metaphysical dogmas may assist its propagation among a certain class of minds. But that class must always be a limited one. Men in general are so constituted that they prefer to take their beliefs upon trust and not to work them out independently: they require teachers, men who speak with authority, as themselves divine, or as direct missionaries of a higher power, or as interpreters of the knowledge slowly accumulated by Humanity in the past. Even granting that each individual would consent to examine himself in order to elicit the requisite first truths, there is no guarantee that the process would be correctly performed in every case, or that the same conclusions would be invariably arrived at. So far as individuals can be induced to agree in their interpretations of self-consciousness, to that extent Brahmoism offers a basis of organisation; but it is obvious that such agreement must always be confined to a comparatively narrow circle of believers. The masses require a less abstract creed, and one that contains a larger infusion of the human element. There are already indications of a modification in this direction; and however much the philosophical party among the progressive Brahmos may disclaim any wish to depart from a purely theistic type of worship, it is certain that such success as they have obtained is at the expense of their theological metaphysics. Instead of trying to controvert this fact, it would be better if they faced it boldly and acknowledged the paramount necessity of grafting the human upon the divine. It is only by accepting such principles and adopting the most liberal modifications, both in doctrine and practice, that Brahmoism can ever hope to spread among the lower or less educated classes. In its present profession it has made no way among the masses of the people. In its present attitude it will never even form a transitional religion enabling the nation to pass through its present crisis: much less will it ever prove a formidable rival to any of the older creeds.

Somewhat similar in its individualistic character is the metaphysical conception of Theosophy which has lately been exercising a transitory influence. The subtleness of its teaching, and the degree of scope which the supernatural interference of spiritual, or so-called astral, phenomena afford to the imagination, are features peculiarly congenial to the Hindoo intellect. A belief in the doctrines of Theosophy is consistent with the tenets of Brahmoism, and even with the professions of orthodox Hindooism. The Indian mind has also been able to see that in some occult manner, but with a definiteness and force quite unmistakable, the European adherents of the system have been elevated by a kind of moral regeneration from indifferentism, and sometimes from positive dislike, into sincere and hearty sympathy with the people of the country. The conditions have, therefore, been very favourable to the spread of Theosophy among natives. Tossed to and fro by every blast of vain doctrine, they have rallied round the newfangled ideas of this weird and obscure system with an eagerness which shows the need among them of a more rational and satisfying belief. But already the enthusiasm of the movement has spent itself. The public exposure of some of the directors of the new cult proved a severe shock to its votaries, and many of them have renounced their allegiance. Although they are full of faith and trust, to an extent which Englishmen of the twentieth century are almost incapable of understanding, they cannot but refuse to remain permanently enslaved by a belief in phenomena which are not only incapable of demonstration, but are alleged on credible testimony to be propped up by fraud.

More valid than these metaphysical tendencies is the advance which has been made, especially in Upper India, of the position and prospects of the Arya Samaj. This movement is the direct outcome of the conservative and reactionary Hindoo feeling which sighs for the visionary Golden Age, and finds the remedy for the defects of modern Hindooism, tainted by its contact with Western civilisation, in the inspiration and glories of the past. It is based, like the Brahmo Samaj, on pure Monotheism, but appeals more strongly to the intellectual Hindoo by its adherence to the philosophy and cosmogony which are familiar to him, while it attracts the masses by its maintenance of the inspired character of their ancient scriptures. "Back to the Vedas" was the persistent cry of Dayanund Saraswati, and the belief in an inspired scripture is a living force to those who are unable to find adequate moral or religious sustenance in the eclectic principles of Ram Mohun Roy or Keshob Chunder Sen. The strength of the movement lies in its indigenous source, with its roots in the past, adhering to the ancient ritual and a modified caste system, and retaining a not unfamiliar attitude in respect of pantheism and idol-worship : its weakness lies in its strained and unnatural interpretation of the sacred books, and above all in its complete alienation from Western thought. There is no blend, or sign of blending, between Aryas and the followers of any other creed, Eastern or Western, thus fundamentally differing from the Theism of the Brahmo Samaj ; and their attitude towards Christianity and Islam is distinctly hostile. It may be in consequence of this attitude that the doctrines of the new sect have rapidly spread, and are already exercising a powerful influence, socially and politically, among large numbers of the people. It is certain that, in spite of its dogmatism, the Arya Samaj is working as a remarkable force for the amelioration of India, and the history of the movement is one of the most important and interesting chapters of modern Hindoo thought.

Absolute Nihilism, Brahmoism, Theosophy, Theism which conforms to Hindooism, and, lastly, Christianity, these generally are the varying creeds which among Hindoos survive the wreck of their early faith. As a rule, the Hindoos retain their religious instincts ; but there are no signs at present of the predominance of any creed. Wandering hither and thither like sheep without a shepherd, they beat the air in the vain pursuit after religious truth. We cannot tell what the future—and doubtless it is a far distant future—is destined to bring forth. But I for one cannot bring myself to doubt that the Eastern nations will some day be brought with the rest of the world under one common faith, towards which all discordant religions will eventually converge. I cannot doubt that by distinct but equivalent courses the great nations of the East will rise by natural progression to the definitive level of the West, and embrace the final universal and human religion which has its roots in man's moral nature—the same in all ages and climes—while it will not fail in each case to reflect the national life and give expression to its distinctive aspirations. Although the prospects of moral progress in India are threatened by gathering clouds, I derive encouragement from a contemplation of the brilliant success attained by evangelists of an earlier generation. No beneficial impulse is likely to be produced by the mere official experiments of a Government which is alien to the people, and which, from no fault of its own, is necessarily unsympathetic with caste and polytheism. The Educational Department possesses no adequate force for revolutionising the thoughts and manners of the people. The missionary bodies are now as incapable as laymen of sympathising with the special idiosyncrasies of the Hindoo intellect. But the admirable efforts of the Jesuit missionaries in China and in Southern India have shown the possibility of surmounting obstacles at first sight fairly insuperable. Had they possessed a more tractable dogma, they would doubtless have overcome the moral difficulty for themselves. Even in their failure they accomplished a great work, and have set an example of procedure that succeeding missionaries must follow.

It is to the labours of St Francis Xavier during the sixteenth century that Indian Christianity is chiefly indebted for its distinctive characteristics. He addressed his teaching almost exclusively to the lower orders, and made no systematic attempt to gain over to his side the aristocracy of Hindooism. A more decisive step was taken in the beginning of the seventeenth century when the celebrated Jesuit, Robert de Nobili, well knowing how important it was to receive the co-operation of the upper classes, commenced his labours, after the manner of St Paul, by becoming a Brahmin to the Brahmins. He and his colleagues assumed Hindoo names and introduced themselves as Brahmin priests of a superior order from the Western world.

Their success was due to their wonderful power of sympathy, and their rare facility of adaptation to unaccustomed modes of thought and action. They possessed in an eminent degree the apostolic faculty of being all things to all men without compromising the fundamental principles of their creed. Like skilful pilots, they steered clear of an absolute enforcement of doctrine, and instinctively adopted a theory of relativity in all their dealings with the social customs and religions of the Eastern world. They displayed, on the one hand, that just conciliation which is the keynote of the principles they had to offer in dealing with other modes of thought; and, on the other, that life of example of which the effect is beyond all precept, and without which all precept is in vain.

. . . . . .

"They renounced all riches, dignities, honours, friends and kindred; they desired to have nothing of this world; they scarcely took the necessaries of life; attention to the body, even when needful, was irksome to them.

. . . . . .

"They were given as an example for all religious, and ought more to excite us to make good progress than should the number of the lukewarm make us grow slack.

. . . . . .

"Their footsteps remaining still bear witness that they were right holy and perfect men, who, waging war so stoutly, trod the world under their feet."

APPENDIX

The Partition of Bengal

I have touched in the body of this work on the secret springs which lay at the root of the scheme for the partition of the Bengal Province, on the unpopularity of the measure, on the defiance of all public opinion in forcing it on the people, and on the profound effect which it has produced in strengthening the national movement, not in Bengal only, but in all parts of India. I have been advised to supplement these remarks, for the benefit of the English reader, with a brief explanation of the administrative reasons put forward for the partition, an examination of those reasons, and a statement of the attitude of the populations concerned in regard to them.

The partition of Bengal cuts the Bengalee nation into two parts, according to a purely arbitrary line. It is based on no ethnical distinctions, and follows no ancient frontier. It divides a province which has been united from the earliest times known to history. It necessitates a decision on the part of two separate administrations and of two separate legislatures on every question concerning the Bengalee people—their land system, their municipal system, their taxation, their police, their communications, and their education. It means the disruption of the nation politically and socially. It is small wonder that the people do not submit to it.

The official justification of the scheme is to be found in the argument that the administration of Bengal, with its population of nearly eighty millions of inhabitants, is a burden too heavy for any one man to bear. The force of this argument must be admitted, and there can be no doubt that the Lieutenant-Governorship of Bengal was a very heavy charge. No one would deny that. At the same time I do not hesitate to say that this argument was unduly pressed. I have served as Under-Secretary to Government, or as Secretary to Government, under seven Lieutenant-Governors, and therefore know something of this matter. The truth is that the charge was a heavier one in former times than lately. I can remember the time when it used to take the Lieutenant-Governor a fortnight to journey to the other end of his province. Now there is no district which he could not get to in one day. Railways have transformed the administration, and their work has been supplemented by the telegraph. Facilities of communication have very much more than compensated a Lieutenant-Governor for the increase of work thrown on him in other directions. Nor must it be forgotten that the people of Bengal are the most easily administered in India. Notwithstanding its enormous preponderance in population, there are fewer criminals in Bengal than in the United Provinces or in Madras. Mere administration is a simple task. It becomes difficult only when we fight against the will of the people, and do not govern through them and with them, but against them.

Still I admit, and have always admitted, that the Lieutenant-Governorship of Bengal was an onerous charge, and that some change in the form of administration was called for. Relief, however, should not have been provided in any such unpopular direction as the partitioning of the province. The Indian public do not desire the development of a "one man rule." Their demand is for the abolition of the two Lieutenant-Governorships of Bengal and of Eastern Bengal, and for the substitution in their place of a Governor appointed from England,

and of an Executive Council of local officials who would relieve the Governor from administrative and legislative details. Leave the province alone, they say, but give us a Governor and a Council. An examination of the Regulating Act of 1833 and of the subsequent Statute of 1833 (16 & 17 Vict. c. 95) will disclose the fact that it was always intended to appoint a Governor in Bengal with an Executive Council, as in Bombay and Madras, and that it is only pending such form of government that the Governor-General is empowered to appoint a Lieutenant-Governor from time to time. The existence of a Lieutenant-Governorship in Bengal is therefore only a provisional arrangement, and the perpetuation of the present system involves the suspension and indefinite postponement of the operation of a Parliamentary Statute by executive authority. The prayer of the Bengalees is not only that there should be no partition, but that the intention of the Statute should be revived, and a Governor and Council established for the whole of the old province.

In the despatch of the Government of India to the Secretary of State (page 8 of Blue Book, cd. 2746) it is stated that the suggestion of "a Council to assist the Lieutenant-Governor of

Bengal has now again been revived, and has been pressed upon us as the sole available alternative to territorial reconstruction." But so far as the people of Bengal are concerned, no such suggestion was ever made. It is a Governor, and not a Lieutenant-Governor, that they want. The despatch goes on, however, to deal with the question of a Governor in Council, and formulates objections to the proposal, which are summed up by Mr Brodrick when he says in his reply, dated 9th of June 1905, that "a strong personal government is in an Asiatic country the most effective form of administration." It is said that a "one man rule" is the best. That is a belated argument, very dear to bureaucrats everywhere, but wholly out of place and retrograde in its application to Bengal, which is the most advanced province in our Indian Empire, and where English ideas, education, and culture have most firmly taken root. The desire of the Bengalee people is emphatically in favour of modifying this "one man rule" policy.

What would follow from the creation of a Governorship and Council? It implies the appointment of a Governor from England of higher position and greater independence than appertains to the office of a Lieutenant-Governor. The policy of the Government of India for some years past has been to lower the prestige and influence of all local governments. The conversion of Governors into Lieutenant-Governors is a part of that policy, the object being to place the nomination to these offices in the hands of the Viceroy, and so to weaken the independence of the Presidency Governments. But the inherent defect in the status of a Lieutenant-Governor is, that he is not in a position to be independent without risking or sacrificing his future prospects. He not only owes his appointment to the Viceroy, but he naturally entertains in his heart a desire to be enshrined in the Council of the Secretary of State for India when he retires. Therefore it is that we shall not find in Lieutenant-Governors selected from the Civil Service in India that firmness and independence which is characteristic of a Governor appointed from England by the Secretary of State. Madras and Bombay are both of them fortunate in the possession of a Governor and Council, and the time has come when a similar system of administration should be extended to Bengal. That is a form of devolution which the circumstances of Bengal now require. It would bring with it greater independence, a stronger government, and improved administration. It would be joyfully and enthusiastically accepted by the populations concerned, as a solution of the problem which has been so much troubling their rulers, but in regard to which their own opinions and desires have been so lamentably ignored. Partition may be "a settled fact," but perhaps it is not too late even now to reconsider it from this point of view. It is the only way, and an easy way, of ensuring widespread popular gratitude, in the place of bitterness and discontent.

One word more with reference to the advisability of affording further relief to the heads of the Administration. It is obvious that the burden of work is much less when distributed between a Governor and Council than when it rests upon the shoulders of a single Lieutenant-Governor, or even of two Lieutenant-Governors. But in so large a province as United Bengal a certain measure of delegation of authority is needed. The amalgamation of Assam with Bengal seems to be necessary under any scheme. But the special conditions of this province, especially in regard to the tea industry and the control over frontier and savage tribes along the north-east boundary of India, appear to render it obligatory to adopt measures of delegating powers to the local Commissioner corresponding to those which, under the Indian Act V. of 1868, may be delegated by the Government of Bombay to the Commissioner in Scinde. It is probable that in the case of Behar also it would be desirable to delegate similar powers to the Commissioner of that division, and this step might possibly be adopted in the case of Orissa. These are details : but it is in this direction that relief could be afforded without disintegrating the province, and without outraging the feelings of the people.

INDEX

Index

Index

Index

Index

Index

Index

Index

Index

Index

Index

Index

Index

PRINTED BY NEILL AND CO., LTD., EDINBURGH.